Anonymous

Heavenly Hymns for Heavy Hearts

Anonymous

Heavenly Hymns for Heavy Hearts

ISBN/EAN: 9783744774857

Printed in Europe, USA, Canada, Australia, Japan

Cover: Foto ©Thomas Meinert / pixelio.de

More available books at **www.hansebooks.com**

FOR

HEAVY HEARTS.

COMPILED FOR
THE PRESBYTERIAN BOARD OF PUBLICATION.

PHILADELPHIA:
PRESBYTERIAN BOARD OF PUBLICATION,
No. 821 Chestnut Street.

Entered according to the Act of Congress, in the year 1864, by

THE TRUSTEES OF THE

PRESBYTERIAN BOARD OF PUBLICATION,

In the Clerk's Office of the District Court for the Eastern District of Pennsylvania.

STEREOTYPED BY WESTCOTT & THOMSON.

INDEX.

	PAGE
After our child's untroubled breath.........*James Russell Lowell.*	103
A little word in kindness spoken..............................*Anonymous.*	57
Alone! ah me! that word alone................................*Sophronia.*	92
Alone I walked the ocean strand.............*Hannah Flagg Gould.*	36
As stars upon the tranquil sea........................*Carlos L. Stuart.*	62
A strange power hath the human heart...*Mrs. Martha Canfield.*	72
Bear the burden of the present..................... *Thomas Mackellar.*	41
Beside the toilsome way...*Anonymous.*	107
Be patient, life is very brief...*Anonymous.*	140
Beyond the smiling and the weeping.............*Horatius Bonar.*	162
Be not harsh and unforgiving....................................*Anonymous.*	19
But to be still, oh but to cease awhile..............*Fanny Kemble.*	100
Calm me, my God, and keep me calm............*Horatius Bonar.*	98
Cease thou from man, oh what to thee...................*Anonymous.*	111
Christian, walk carefully, danger is near..............*Anonymous.*	30
Child of sorrow, lone, forsaken....................................*Anonymous.*	48
Come, my soul, thou must be waking..........*Baron Von Canitz.*	26
Come to me, Lord, when first I wake....................*Anonymous.*	119
Count each affliction, whether light or grave..........*Anonymous.*	118
Cling to the Crucified..................................*Horatius Bonar.*	137
Dear little child, with thy golden hair......................*Anonymous.*	193
Drops of honey, let them fall...................................*Mrs. Anger.*	47

3

INDEX.

	PAGE
Each hour is like an angel that with wings.....*John G. Whittier.*	209
Early my spirit turned................................*James W. Alexander.*	40
Faint not beneath thy burden, though it seem..........*Anonymous.*	206
Father, I know that all my life...............*Mrs. Waring.*	112
For ever the sun is pouring his gold ....*Anonymous.*	186
Forsake me not, my God.......................*From the German.*	37
For what shall I praise Thee, my God and my King...*Mrs. Fry.*	108
Fighting the battle of life...........................*Anonymous.*	86
Go labour on! spend and be spent!...............*Horatius Bonar.*	12
"Go forth," said the heavenly Father..........*Mrs. S. W. Jewett.*	211
Half a wreck by tempest driven..................*Anonymous.*	160
Here, in thy presence, Lord, I stand............*Horatius Bonar.*	17
How blessed from the bonds of sin.......................*Spitta*	109
He leadeth me! Oh, blessed thought..............*Anonymous.*	123
He sendeth sun, He sendeth shower..........*Mrs. Sarah F. Adams.*	71
Here in the body pent........................*James Montgomery.*	139
How few, who, from their youthful day..............*Anonymous.*	203
How many forms it shows to us.....................*Anonymous.*	55
Hush, idle words and thoughts of ill.................*Anonymous.*	14
Hues of the rich unfolding morn....................*John Keble.*	31
I am not afraid of dying...........................*Anonymous.*	171
I am old and blind...............................*Elizabeth Lloyd.*	191
I ask not human greatness...............*Mrs. Mary B. Crocker.*	119
I come to Thee, to-night....................*Hymns of the Ages.*	179
I ask not now for gold to gild................*John G. Whittier.*	190
I am weary of straying, oh fain would I rest........*Anonymous.*	74
I'm bound to the house of my Father.......*Hannah Flagg Gould.*	143
I am footsore and very weary...............*Adelaide Anne Proctor.*	141
I cry for peace, O God.............................*Anonymous.*	105
If grief in heaven might find a place ....*Anonymous.*	24

INDEX.

	PAGE
I have done at length with dreaming.......*Anonymous.*	11
I know not the way I am going........*Anonymous.*	124
I'll spare all useless thinking........*Anonymous.*	154
In the dim recess of thy spirit's chamber......*Puritan Recorder.*	194
In the name of God advancing........*From the German.*	178
In youth I died, in maiden bloom......*Anonymous.*	146
I shine in the light of God........*Anonymous.*	167
Is this a time for moonlight dreams?......*John Keble.*	13
Is this the way, my Father? 'Tis my child......*Anonymous.*	169
Is thy lot lonely, fear it not, for He......*Anonymous.*	156
I thank Thee, Father, that I live........*Anonymous.*	10
I thought 'twas Thine to give me, and I craved......*Anonymous.*	94
It is not much the world can give......*Anonymous.*	52
It was a time of sadness, and my heart......*Anonymous.*	196
I will never, never, leave Thee......*Anonymous.*	166
I worship Thee, sweet will of God......*Frederick Faber.*	78
Just as a mother, with sweet pious face......*Anonymous.*	99
Let me not die before I've done for Thee......*Anonymous.*	35
Let us draw their mantles o'er us......*Anonymous.*	54
Life is onward! use it........*Anonymous.*	28
Live to do good, but not with thought......*George W. Bethune.*	16
Look and listen, look and listen......*Anonymous.*	121
Lord, I am come alone with Thee......*Anonymous.*	135
Lo the lilies of the field......*Bishop Heber.*	151
Loving word, and kindly deed......*Anonymous.*	120
Make use of me, my God......*Horatius Bonar.*	80
Must I my brother keep......*Raffles.*	65
My Dove! The Bridegroom speaks, to whom......*Anonymous.*	44
My feet are worn and weary with the march......*S. Roberts.*	89
My God, my Father, while I stray......*Charlotte Elliott.*	116
My God, is any hour so sweet......*Charlotte Elliott.*	138

INDEX.

	PAGE
No shadows yonder............*Horatius Bonar.*	83
No sickness there............*Anonymous.*	170
Not here, not here, not where the sparkling...*Congregationalist.*	199
Now the crucible is breaking............*Harttman.*	90
Nothing but leaves............*Christian Inquirer.*	158
Oh be ye thankful while ye breathe............*Anonymous.*	148
O dearest Lord, I cannot pray............*Frederick Faber.*	84
O fainting soul, arise and sing............*John Keble.*	150
Of all the thoughts of God............*Elizabeth Barrett Browning.*	209
Oh! for the happy days gone by............*Frederick Faber.*	75
Oh God of glory! Thou hast treasured up............*Anonymous.*	54
Oh strew on life's wild path a flower............*Anonymous.*	49
Oh! lead me in Thy perfect way............*Anonymous.*	165
Oh! how I fear Thee, living God............*Frederick Faber.*	188
Oh! it is hard to work for God............*Frederick Faber.*	67
Oh! never till the clouds of time............*James Montgomery.*	207
Oh! let the soul its slumbers break............*Spanish Poem.*	144
Oh! leave a smile of kindness............*Anonymous.*	52
One by one, the sands are flowing............*Adelaide Anne Proctor.*	48
One hour with Thee, my God, when daylight............*Anonymous.*	133
One little word, if softly spoken............*Julian Cramer.*	42
One sweetly solemn thought............*Carey.*	81
Only waiting till the shadows............*Anonymous.*	157
Oh! to be ready............*Anonymous.*	151
Our beloved have departed............*From the German of Lange.*	175
Pain's furnace heat within me quivers............*Sturm.*	130
Purer yet, and purer............*Anonymous.*	164
Ready now to spread my pinions............*Anonymous.*	155
Shall this life of mine be wasted............*Horatius Bonar.*	39
Speak gently to the little child............*Maria Roseau.*	66
Speechless Sorrow sat with me............*Harriet McEwen Kimball.*	125

INDEX.

		PAGE
Soul, be strong, whate'er betide	*Martin Farquhar Tupper.*	96
Sweet brooklet, ever gliding	*Sir Robert Grant.*	22

Tarry with me, O my Saviour	*Anonymous.*	127
That clime is not like this dull clime of ours	*Horatius Bonar.*	161
The cricket, he dwells in the cold, cold ground	*Hadassah.*	59
The God of glory walks His rounds	*Bishop Heber.*	25
The heavier the cross, the nearer heaven	*German of Schmolk.*	131
The sympathy of Jesus	*Margaret Junkin.*	20
Throw away Thy rod	*Herbert.*	106
Then, oh have pity, Father, on thy child	*Fannie Raymond.*	145
There is a little mystic clock	*From the German.*	34
The night is mother of the day	*Anonymous.*	51
There is an eye that never sleeps	*From Gems of Eng. Poetry.*	115
There is no pain that I can bear	*Anonymous.*	205
There was an idle lyre	*Margaret Junkin.*	101
This world, O God, like that above	*Madame Guyon.*	115
They err, who measure life by years	*Abby Allen.*	33
Thou knowest my weakness, Lord, my every	*Anonymous.*	126
Thy way, not mine, O Lord	*Horatius Bonar.*	129
Time and Patience, these are angels	*Anonymous.*	134
Time is flying, flying	*Anonymous.*	152
'Tis a little thing	*Talfourd.*	54
'Tis not for us to trifle! Life is brief	*Horatius Bonar.*	9
'Tis first the true, and then the beautiful	*Horatius Bonar.*	159
To be the thing we seem	*Horæ Poeticæ.*	183
True faith, producing love to God and man	*Anonymous.*	63
Till He come, oh let the words	*Rev. E. H. Bickersteth.*	189

| Very many are the blessings | *Anonymous.* | 56 |
| Voyager on life's troubled sea | *Anonymous.* | 113 |

| Wait, for the day is breaking | *Chauncey Hare Townshend.* | 205 |

		PAGE
We all might do good	*Anonymous.*	53
Weep not for those whose race is run	*Anonymous.*	176
We speak of the realms of the blest	*Anonymous.*	177
We walked by the side of the tranquil stream	*Caroline Fry.*	61
Whatever passes as a cloud between	*Anonymous.*	59
What if the little rain should say	*George W. Cutter.*	15
What have I yet to do	*Anonymous.*	184
What no human eye hath seen	*From the German of Lange.*	181
What superscription, oh my soul	*Anonymous.*	118
Where the faded flower shall freshen	*Horatius Bonar.*	173
Who blesses others in his daily deeds	*Anonymous.*	53
Without haste and without rest	*German of Goethe.*	51
Words are lighter than the cloud foam	*Household Words.*	201
Wouldst thou win the crime-stained wanderer	*Anonymous.*	58
We wreathed about our darling's head	*Mrs. Lowell.*	214
Yes, our griefs will soon be over	*Theological Student of Geneva.*	154
Yes, pray for those thou lovest	*Mrs. Addy.*	70
Yet, will I trust, in all my fears	*Martin F. Tupper.*	97

HEAVENLY HYMNS.

OUR ONE LIFE.

'Tis not for us to trifle! Life is brief,
      And sin is here.
Our age is but the falling of a leaf,
      A dropping tear.
We have no time to sport away the hours,
All must be earnest in a world like ours.

Not many lives, but only one have we—
      One, only one;—
How sacred should that one life ever be—
      That narrow span!
Day after day, filled up with blessed toil;
Hour after hour, still bringing in new spoil.

O life below—how brief, and poor, and sad;—
      One heavy sigh.
O. life above—how long, how fair, and glad;
      And endless joy.
Soon we'll be done with daily dying here;
Then will begin the living in yon sphere!

                  HORATIUS BONAR.

'TIS GOOD TO LIVE.

I THANK thee, Father, that I live!
I thank for these gifts of thine,—
For bending skies of heavenly blue,
    And stars divine!

For this green earth, where wild, sweet airs,
Like forest spirits, joyous play:
For winding stream, and trees, and flowers,
    Beside its way.

But more I thank thee for true hearts,
That bear sweet gifts of love to me,
Whom mine enfolds, and feels that this
    Is love of thee.

Warm from their spirits, spreads around
An atmosphere, serene, divine,
Magnetical, like golden haze,
    Encircling mine.

To-day I bless thee most for power,—
It draws me, Father, nearest thee,—
To love all thine, e'en though they give
    No love to me.

In stillness deep, I walk a land
Where spirit-forms my footsteps greet,
And beauteous thoughts, an angel band,
    Chant low, and sweet.

Drear hours, I know, will darkly come,
Like April days of cloud and rain;
But thus must hearts, like wintry fields,
          Grow green again!

I thank thee, Father, that I live!
Though wailings fill this earth of thine;
To labour for thy suffering ones
          Is joy divine.

And even I, so weak and poor,
May bear some word of life from thee;
A beam of hope may reach some heart
          Even through me.
                  Anon.

CONSECRATION.

I HAVE done at length with dreaming,
    Henceforth, O thou soul of mine,
Thou must take up sword and gauntlet
    Waging warfare most divine.
Life is struggle, combat, victory!
    Wherefore have I slumbered on—
With my forces all unmarshalled,
    With my weapons all undrawn?
Oh how many a glorious record,
    Had the angels of me kept,
Had I done, instead of doubted,
    Had I walked instead of crept!

Yet, my soul, look not behind thee,
　　Thou hast work to do at last;
Let the brave toil of the present
　　Over-arch thy crumbling past—
Build thy great acts high, and higher,
　　Build them on the conquered sod,
Where thy weakness first fell bleeding,
　　Where thy first prayer was to God.

Anon.

"MY SOUL, MY SOUL, ARISE! WHY SLEEPEST THOU?"

Go labour on,—spend, and be spent—
　　Thy joy to do thy Father's will;
It is the way the Master went,—
　　Should not the servant tread it still?

Go labour on; 'tis not for nought,—
　　Thy earthly loss is heavenly gain;
Men heed thee, love thee, praise thee not,—
　　Thy Master praises, what are men?

Go labour on; enough, while here,
　　If He shall praise thee; if He deign
Thy willing heart to mark and cheer;
　　No toil for Him shall be in vain.

Toil on, faint not,—keep watch, and pray;
　　Be wise, the erring soul to win;

Go forth into the world's highway,
   Compel the wanderer to come in.

Toil on—and in thy toil rejoice;
   For toil comes rest—for exile home;
Soon shalt thou hear the Bridegroom's voice,
   The midnight peal—"Behold, I come!"
HORATIUS BONAR.

SELF-DENIAL.

Is this a time for moonlight dreams
Of love and home, by many streams?
For fancy, with her shadowy toys,
Aerial hopes, and pensive joys,
While souls are wandering far and wide,
And curses swarm on every side?

No! rather steel thy melting heart
To act the martyr's sternest part,
To watch with firm, unshrinking eye,
Thy darling visions, as they die;
Till all bright hopes, and hues of day
Have faded into twilight gray.

Yes, let them pass without a sigh;
And if the world seem dull and dry,
If long and sad thy lonely hours,
And winds have rent thy sheltering bowers,

Bethink thee what thou art, and where,—
A sinner, in a life of care.

Pray only that thy aching heart,
From visions vain, content to part,
Strong, for love's sake, its woe to hide,
May cheerful wait, the cross beside,
Too happy, if that dreadful day,
Thy life be given thee for a prey.

Snatched sudden from the avenging rod,
Safe in the bosom of thy God,
How wilt thou then look back and smile
On thoughts that bitterest seemed erewhile;
And bless the pangs that made thee see
This was no world of rest for thee!

JOHN KEBLE.

ARISE.

Hush, idle words, and thoughts of ill,
Your Lord is listening, peace, be still!
Christ watches by a Christian's breath—
Be silent, vain deluding mirth,
Till in thine altered voice be known,
Somewhat of resignation's tone.
But chiefly ye should lift your gaze
Above the world's uncertain haze,
And look with calm, unwavering eye,
On the bright fields beyond the sky.

Think not of rest, though dreams be sweet;
Start up and fly your heavenward feet,—
Is not God's oath upon your head
Ne'er to sink back on slothful bed?
Never again your loins untie,
Nor let your torches waste and die,—
Till, when the shadows thickest fall,
Ye hear your Master's midnight call.
Anon.

INFLUENCE.

What if the little rain should say,
  "So small a drop as I
Can ne'er refresh those thirsty fields,
  I'll tarry in the sky?"

What if a shining beam of noon
  Should in its fountain stay,
Because its feeble light alone,
  Cannot create a day?

Doth not each rain-drop help to form
  The cool refreshing shower?
And every ray of light to warm
  And beautify the flower?

Go then—and strive to do thy share;
  One talent—less than thine—
Improved with steady zeal and care,
  Would gain rewards divine.
George W. Cutter.

LIVE TO DO GOOD.

Live to do good; but not with thought to win
  From man return of any kindness done;
Remember Him who died on cross for sin,
  The merciful, the meek, rejected One;
When He was slain for crime of doing good,
Canst thou expect return of gratitude?

Do good to all; but while thou servest best
  And at thy greatest cost, nerve thee to bear,
When thine own heart with anguish is oppressed,
  The cruel taunt, the cold averted air,
From lips which thou hast taught in hope to pray,
And eyes, whose sorrows thou hast wiped away.

Still do thou good; but for His holy sake
  Who died for thine; fixing thy purpose ever
High as His throne no wrath of man can shake;
  So shall he own thy generous endeavour,
And take thee to His conqueror's glory up,
When thou hast shared the Saviour's bitter cup.

Do nought but good; for such the noble strife
  Of virtue is, 'gainst wrong to venture love,
And for thy foe devote a brother's life,
  Content to wait the recompense above;
Brave for the truth, to fiercest insult meek,
In mercy strong, in vengeance only weak.
George W. Bethune.

HERE IS MY HEART.

Here, in thy presence, Lord, I stand;
  I give myself, my all to thee;
Thou hast redeemed me by thy precious blood;
  Thine only will I be.
No love but thine, but thine, can me relieve,
No light but thine, but thine, will I receive,
    No light, no love, but thine!

Take, take me, as I am; thou need'st me not,
  I know thou need'st me not at all;—
All heaven is thine, all earth, each morning star;
  High angels wait thy call;
I am the poorest of thy creatures, I,
The child of evil, and dark misery;—
    Yet take me as I am!

Perhaps thou overlookest me; too small
  A mote of being for thine eye
To rest on, or to care for; far beneath
  Thy mighty majesty.
But still I am a thing of life, I know,
And made for everlasting joy or woe;—
    Turn not thine eye away.

Perhaps thou dost repent of making me?
  And yet this, O my God, I know,
That I am made, made by thine own great hand,
  Though least of all below;

Myself I cannot alter or unmake,
Oh! wilt thou not this soul of mine new make,
   New make me, O my God!

Perhaps for aught of good I am unfit,
   Most worthless, and most useless all;
Yet make me but the meanest thing that lives
   Within thy Salem's wall.
I shall be well content, my God, to be,
Or do or suffer aught that pleaseth thee :—
   Oh! cast me not away!

It would not cost thee dear to bless me, Lord,
   A word would do it, or a sign,
It needs no more from thee, no more, my God;
   Thy words have power divine.
And oh the boundless blessedness to me—
Loved, saved, forgiven, renewed and blessed by thee!
   Oh speak, oh speak the word!

Life ebbs apace, my night is coming fast;
   My cheek is wan, my hair is gray;
I am not what I was, when on me blazed
   The noon of youth's bright day.
Make haste to do for me what thus I plead,
Oh thou the succourer of my great need,
   Oh love and comfort me!

I know the blood of thine eternal Son
   Has power to cleanse even me;

Oh wash me now, in that all-precious blood;
  Give my soul purity;
Scatter the darkness, bid the day-star shine,
Light up the midnight of this soul of mine;
    Let all be song and joy.

HORATIUS BONAR.

LIVE IN LOVE.

BE not harsh and unforgiving,
Live in love, 'tis pleasant living.
If an angry man should meet thee,
And assail thee indiscreetly,
Turn not thou again and rend him,
Lest thou needlessly offend him;
Show him love hath been thy teacher,
Kindness is a potent preacher:
Gentleness is e'er forgiving—
Live in love, 'tis pleasant living.

Why be angry with each other?
Man was made to love his brother;
Kindness is a human duty,
Meekness a celestial beauty.
Words of kindness, spoke in season,
Have a weight with men of reason;
Don't be others' follies blaming,
And their little vices naming;

Charity's a cure for railing,
Suffers much, is all-prevailing;
Courage, then, and be forgiving;
Live in love, 'tis pleasant living.

Let thy loving be a passion,
Not a complimental fashion;
Live in wisdom, ever proving
True philosophy is loving.
Hast thou known that bitter feeling,
Gendered by our hate's concealing;
Better love, though ere so blindly,
E'en thy foes will call it kindly.
Words are wind: O let them never
Friendship's golden love-cord sever!
Nor be angry though another
Scorn to call thee friend or brother;
"Brother," say, "let's be forgiving;
Live in love, 'tis pleasant living."

Anon.

THE SYMPATHY OF JESUS.

The sympathy of Jesus—who
 That ever sobbed one sorrowing moan
On some kind bosom, fondly true,
 Some human bosom like our own,

And felt how much those lips close pressed,
    That hand close clasped could calm our fears,
Can turn to this far tenderer breast,
    Without a gush of thankful tears?

The earthly heart on which we lean
    May have its separate griefs to bear,
Griefs, though unspoken and unseen,
    Yet rankling all the deeper there.
Its faltering strength may scarce sustain
    The torture of its own distress,
And still we add our burdened pain,
    Unconscious how the weight may press.

But He whose human feet have trod
    Earth's hills and valleys—He who knew
No sympathy but that of God,
    Though linked with all that craved it, too—
Knows all our yearning, all our need,
    Yet strong to bear our utmost smart—
He loves to feel the throbbing head
    Close laid against His pitying heart.

To think that on the throne of thrones
    He wears our lowly nature still!
To think that midst the loftiest tones
    That through the eternal mansions thrill,
Earth's humblest pleader He will hear,
    Though only tears his anguish tell;
That sobbing voice falls on His ear
    More sweet than Gabriel's ever fell.

Then, sorrowing spirit, take the grief
    Thou ne'er to mortal couldst disclose,
And He will give thee sure relief,
    Touched with the feeling of thy woes;
And thou shalt understand how sweet,
    How filled with more than human bliss,
How dear—how tender—how complete
    The sympathy of Jesus is!
MARGARET JUNKIN.

SWEET BROOKLET.

Sweet brooklet, ever gliding,
Now high the mountain riding,
The lone vale now dividing,
    Whither away!
"With pilgrim course I flow,
Or in summer's scorching glow,
Or o'er moorless wastes of snow,
    Nor stop nor stay;
For, oh! by high behest,
To a bright abode of rest
In my Parent Ocean's breast
    I hasten away."

Many a dark morass,
Many a craggy pass,
Thy feeble force must pass:—
    Yet, yet delay!

"Though the marsh be dire and deep
Though the crag be stern and steep,
On, on, my course must sweep,—
　　I may not stay:
For, oh! be it east or west,
To a home of glorious rest,
In the bright sea's boundless breast,
　　I hasten away."

The warbling bowers beside thee,
The laughing flowers that hide thee,—
With soft accord, they chide thee,
　　Sweet brooklet stay.
"I taste of the fragrant flowers;
I respond to the warbling bowers,
And sweetly they charm the hours
　　Of my winding way;
But ceaseless still, in quest
Of that everlasting rest,
In my parent's boundless breast,
　　I hasten away."

Knowest thou that dread abyss?
Is it a scene of bliss?
Ah, rather cling to this,
　　Sweet brooklet stay!
"Oh, who shall fitly tell
What wonders there may dwell?
That world of mystery well
　　Might strike dismay.

But I know 'tis my parent's breast,—
There held, I must needs be blest;
And with joy, to that promised rest,
    I hasten away."

Sir Robert Grant.

A STARLESS CROWN.

" It would be a sad thing to wear a starless crown in heaven."

If grief in heaven might find a place,
  And shame the worshipper bow down,
Who meets the Saviour face to face,
  'Twould be to wear a starless crown!

Nor find in all that countless host
  We meet before the eternal throne,
Who once like us were sinners lost,
  Any to say, we led them home!

The Son, to do his Father's will,
  Could lay his own bright crown aside;
The law's stern mandate to fulfil—
  Poured out his blood for us and died!

Shall we, who know his wondrous love,
  While here below sit idly down?
Ah then,—if we reach heaven above,
  There'll be for us a starless crown!

Oh may it ne'er of me be said,
  No soul that's saved by grace divine,
Has called for blessings on my head,
  Or linked her destiny with mine.
Anon.

"WHY STAND YE IDLE?"

The God of glory walks his round,
  From day to day, from year to year,
And warns us each with awful sound,
  "No longer stand ye idle here.

"Ye whose young cheeks are rosy bright,
  Whose hands are strong, whose hearts are clear,
Waste not of hope the morning light!
  Ah, fools! why stand ye idle here?

"Oh, as the griefs ye would assuage,
  That wait on life's declining year,
Secure a blessing for your age,
  And work your Master's business here!

"One hour remains, there is but one!
  But many a shriek and many a tear
Through endless years the guilt must moan,
  Of moments lost and wasted here!"

Oh Thou, by all thy works adored,
  To whom the sinner's soul is dear,
Recall us to thy vineyard, Lord!
  And grant us grace to please thee here!
Bishop Heber.

A MORNING HYMN.

Come, my soul, thou must be waking—
Now is breaking
  O'er the earth another day;
Come to Him who made this splendour—
See thou render
  All thy feeble powers can pay.

From the stars thy course be learning;
Dimly burning,
  'Neath the sun, their light grows pale:
So let all that sense delighted,
While benighted,
  From God's presence fade and fail.

Lo! how all of breath partaking,
Gladly waking,
  Hail the sun's enlivening light!
Plants, whose life mere sap doth nourish,
Rise and flourish,
  When he breaks the shades of night.

Thou, too, hail the light returning—
Ready burning
  Be the incense of thy powers;
For the night is safely ended—
God hath tended
  With his care, thy helpless hours.

Pray that He may prosper ever
Each endeavour,
   When thine aim is good and true,
But that he may ever thwart thee,
And convert thee,
   When thou evil wouldst pursue.

Think that He thy ways beholdeth—
He unfoldeth
   Every fault that lurks within;
Every stain of shame glossed over,
Can discover,
   And discern each deed of sin.

Fettered to the fleeting hours
All our powers,
   Vain and brief, are borne away.
Time, my soul, thy ship is steering,
Onward veering,
   To the gulf of death a prey.

Mayst thou, then, on life's last morrow,
Free from sorrow,
   Pass away in slumber sweet;
And, released from death's dark sadness,
Rise in gladness,
   That far brighter Sun to greet.

Only God's free gifts abuse not,
His light refuse not,
   But still his Spirit's voice obey;

Soon shall joy thy brow be wreathing,
Splendour breathing
  Fairer than the fairest day.

If aught of care this morn oppress thee,
To Him address thee,
  Who, like the sun, is good to all.
He gilds the mountain tops, the while
His gracious smile
  Will on the humblest fall.

Round thee, gifts His bounty showers;
Walls and towers
  Girt with flames, thy God shall rear;
Angel legions, to defend thee,
Shall attend thee—
  Hosts whom Satan's self shall fear.

BARON VON CANITZ.

LIFE.

LIFE is onward: use it
  With a forward aim;
Toil is heavenly—choose it,
  And its warfare claim.
Look not to another
  To perform your will;
Let not your own brother
  Keep your warm hand still.

Life is onward: never
   Look upon the past;
It would hold you ever
   In its clutches fast.
Now is your dominion,
   Weave it as you please.
Bind not the soul's pinion
   To a bed of ease.

Life is onward: try it,
   Ere the day is lost;
It hath virtue, buy it,
   At whatever cost.
If the world should offer
   Every precious gem,
Look not at the scoffer,
   Change it not for them.

Life is onward: heed it
   In each varied dress;
Your own act can speed it
   On to happiness.
His bright pinion o'er you
   Time waves not in vain,
If Hope chant before you
   Her prophetic strain.

Life is onward: prize it
   In sunshine and in storm;
Oh! do not despise it
   In its humblest form.

Hope and Joy together,
Standing at the goal,
Through life's darkest weather
Beckon on the soul.

Anon.

THE CHRISTIAN'S WALK.

CHRISTIAN! walk *carefully*—danger is near,
On, in thy journey, with trembling and fear;
Snares from without and temptations within,
Seek to entice thee again into sin.

Christian! walk *cheerfully* — though the fierce storm,
Darken the sky with the clouds of alarm,
Soon will those clouds and the tempest be past,
And thou shalt dwell safely with Jesus at last.

Christian! walk *humbly*—exult not in pride;
All that thou hast is by Jesus supplied;
Holding thee up, he directeth thy ways,
To him be for ever the glory and praise.

Christian! walk *steadfastly*—while in the light;
Swift are approaching the shadows of night!
All that thy Master hath bidden thee, do,
Haste to perform, for thy moments are few!

Christian! walk *prayerfully*—oft wilt thou fall,
If thou forget on thy Saviour to call:
But safe shalt thou walk through each trial and
    care,
If thou art clad in the armour of prayer.

Christian! walk *hopefully*—trouble and pain
Cease when the haven of rest thou dost gain.
This from the lips of the Judge, thy reward:—
"Enter for ever the joy of thy Lord!"
Anon.

MORNING.

"His compassions fail not. They are new every morning."
Lament. iii. 22, 23.

Hues of the rich unfolding morn,
That, ere the glorious sun be born,
By some soft touch invisible
Around his path are taught to swell:—

Why waste your treasures of delight
Upon our thankless, joyless sight,
Who, day by day, to sin awake,
Seldom of heaven and you partake?

Oh! timely happy, timely wise,
Hearts that with rising morn arise!
Eyes that the beam celestial view,
Which evermore makes all things new!

New every morning is the love
Our wakening and uprising prove;
Through sleep and darkness safely brought,
Restored to life, and power, and thought.

New mercies, each returning day,
Hover around us, while we pray;
New perils past, new sins forgiven,
New thoughts of God, new hopes of heaven.

If on our daily course, our mind
Be set, to hallow all we find,
New treasures still, of countless price,
God will provide for sacrifice.

We need not bid, for cloistered cell,
Our neighbour and our work farewell,
Nor strive to wind ourselves too high
For sinful man beneath the sky:

The trivial round, the common task,
Would furnish all we ought to ask;—
Room to deny ourselves; a road
To bring us daily, nearer God.

Only, O Lord, in thy dear love
Fit us for perfect rest above;
And help us, this, and every day,
To live more nearly as we pray.

JOHN KEBLE.

THE LIFE-GAUGE.

They err who measure life by years,
    With false or thoughtless tongue:
Some hearts grow old before their time;
    Others are always young!

'Tis not the number of the lines
    On life's fast filling page;
'Tis not the pulse's added throbs,
    Which constitute our age.

Some souls are serfs, among the free,
    While others nobly strive;
They stand just where their fathers stood;
    Dead, even while they live!

Others, all spirit, heart and sense;—
    Their's the mysterious power
To live, in thrills of joy or wo,
    A twelvemonth in an hour!

Seize, then, the minutes as they pass—
    The wolf of life is *thought;*
Warm up the colours, let them glow,
    By fire or fancy fraught!

Live to some purpose—make thy life
    A gift of use to thee—
A joy, a good, a golden hope,
    A heavenly argosy!

                      Abby Allin.

THE LIFE-CLOCK.

There is a little mystic clock,
    No human eye hath seen,
That beateth on—and beateth on,
    From morning until e'en.

And when the soul is wrapped in sleep,
    And heareth not a sound;
It ticks and ticks, the live-long night,
    And never runneth down.

Oh, wondrous is the work of art,
    Which knells the passing hour,—
But art ne'er formed, nor mind conceived,
    The life-clock's magic power.

Nor set in gold, nor decked with gems,
    By pride and wealth possessed,
But rich or poor, or high, or low,
    Each bears it in his breast.

When life's deep stream 'mid beds of flowers,
    And still, and softly glides;
Like the wavelet's step, with a gentle beat,
    It warns of passing tides.

When passion nerves the warrior's arm
    For deeds of hate and wrong,
Though heeded not, the fearful sound,
    The knell is deep and strong.

When eyes to eyes are gazing soft,
    And tender words are spoken,
Then fast and wild, it rattles on,
    As if with love 'twere broken.

Such is the clock that measures
    Of flesh and spirit blended,
And thus 'twill run within the breast,
    Till this strange life is ended.
From the German.

MY PRAYER.

Let me not die before I've done for Thee
My earthly work, whatever it may be;
Call me not hence, with mission unfulfilled,
Let me not leave my space of ground untilled.
Impress this truth upon me—that not one
Can do my portion, that I leave undone;—
For each one, in thy vineyard, hath a spot
To labour in, for life, and weary not.
Then give me strength, all faithfully to toil,
Converting barren earth to fruitful soil.
I long to be an instrument of Thine,
To be the means one human soul to save
From the dark terrors of a hopeless grave.
Yet most I want a spirit of content,
To work where'er thou'lt wish my labour spent,
Whether at home, or in a stranger clime,—
In days of joy, or sorrow's sterner time;

I want a spirit, passive to lie still
And by thy power to do Thy holy will.
And when this prayer unto my lips doth rise,—
"Before a new home doth my soul surprise"
Let me accomplish some great work for Thee!
Subdue it, Lord! let my petition be:—
"Oh make me useful in this land of Thine.
In ways according to thy will, not mine."
Let me not leave my space of ground untilled,
Call me not hence with mission unfulfilled,
Let me not die before I've done for Thee
My earthly work, whatever it may be!

Anon.

A NAME IN THE SAND.

Alone I walked the ocean strand,
A pearly shell was in my hand;
I stooped, and wrote upon the sand
    My name—the year—the day,
As onward from the spot I passed;
One lingering look behind I cast—
A wave came rolling high and fast,
    And washed my lines away.

And so, methought, 'twill shortly be
With every mark on earth from me;
A wave of dark oblivion's sea
    Will sweep across the place

Where I have trod the sandy shore
Of time, and been, to be no more;
Of me, my frame, the name I bore,
    To leave no track nor trace.

And yet, with Him who counts the sands,
And holds the waters in His hands,
I know a lasting record stands
    Inscribed against my name,
Of all this mortal part has wrought,
Of all this thinking soul has thought,
And from these fleeting moments caught
    For glory or for shame!
                HANNAH F. GOULD.

GOD'S SUPPORT AND GUIDANCE.

FORSAKE me not, my God,
    Thou God of my salvation!
Give me thy light, to be
    My sure illumination.
My soul to folly turns,
    Seeking, she knows not what;
Oh! lead her to thyself—
    My God, forsake me not!

Forsake me not, my God!
    Take not thy Spirit from me;
And suffer not the might
    Of sin to overcome me.

A father pitieth
  The children he begot;
My Father, pity me—
  My God, forsake me not.

Forsake me not, my God!
  Thou God of life and power,
Enliven, strengthen me
  In every evil hour;
And when the sinful fire
  Within my heart is hot,
Be not thou far from me,—
  My God, forsake me not!

Forsake me not, my God!
  Uphold me in my going,
That evermore I may
  Please thee in all well-doing;
And that thy will, O Lord!
  May never be forgot
In all my works and ways—
  My God, forsake me not!

Forsake me not, my God!
  I would be thine for ever;
Confirm me mightily
  In every right endeavour:
And when my hour is come,
  Cleansed from all stain and spot
Of sin, receive my soul—
  My God, forsake me not!

From the German.

FORWARD.

Shall this life of mine be wasted?
    Shall this vineyard lie untilled?
Shall true joy pass by untasted,
    And this soul remain unfilled?

Shall this heart still spend its treasures
    On the things that fade and die?
Shall it count the hollow pleasures
    Of bewildering vanity?

Shall these lips of mine be idle—
    Shall I open them in vain?
Shall I not with God's own bridle
    Their frivolities restrain?

Shall these eyes of mine still wander?
    Or, no longer turned afar,
Fix a firmer gaze, and fonder,
    On the bright and Morning Star?

Shall these feet of mine, delaying,
    Still in ways of sin be found,
Braving snares, and madly straying
    On the world's bewitching ground?

No! I was not born to trifle
    Life away, in dreams of sin.
No! I was not born to stifle
    Longings such as these within.

Where the cross, God's love revealing,
   Sets the fettered spirit free;
Where it sheds the wondrous healing,
   There, my soul, thy rest shall be.

Then, no longer idly dreaming,
   Shall I fling my years away;
But each precious hour redeeming,
   Wait for the eternal day.

HORATIUS BONAR.

GOD, MY EXCEEDING JOY.

Psalm xliii. 4.

EARLY my spirit turned
   From earthly things away,
And agonized and yearned
   For the eternal day:
Dimly I saw when but a boy,
God, my exceeding joy.

In days of fiercer flame,
   When passion urged me on
'Twas only bliss in name—
   The pleasure soon was gone.
Compared with Thee how all things cloy,
God, my exceeding joy!

At length the moment came—
   Jesus made known his love;

High shot the kindling flame
   To glories all above,
Now all the powers one theme employ,
God, my exceeding joy.

Shadows came on apace;
   Tears were a pensive shower;
I cried for timely grace
   To save me from the hour:
Thou gavest peace, without alloy;
God, my exceeding joy.

One trial yet awaits,
   Gigantic at the close;
All that my spirit hates
   May then my peace oppose;
But God shall this last foe destroy,—
God, my exceeding joy.
                JAMES W. ALEXANDER.

PATIENT CONTINUANCE IN WELL-DOING.

BEAR the burden of the present—
   Let the morrow bear its own;
If the morning sky be pleasant,
   Why the coming night bemoan?

If the darkened heavens lower,
   Wrap thy cloak around thy form;

Though the tempest rise in power,
    God is mightier than the storm!

Steadfast faith, and hope unshaken
    Animate the trusting breast;
Step by step, the journey's taken,
    Nearer to the land of rest!

All unseen, the Master walketh
    By the toiling servant's side;
Comfortable words he talketh,
    While his hands uphold and guide.

Grief, nor pain, nor any sorrow,
    Rends thy breast to him unknown;
He to-day, and he to-morrow,
    Grace sufficient gives his own.

Holy strivings nerve and strengthen—
    Long endurance wins the crown;
When the evening's shadows lengthen,
    Thou shalt lay the burden down!
Thomas Mackellar.

KIND WORDS.

One little word, if softly spoken—
    One little tear, if kindly shed—
Can heal the spirit bruised and broken,
    And cure the heart that long hath bled.

Once in a distant land, a stranger—
   Alike unknowing, and unknown—
A prey to every hidden danger—
   I wandered darkly on alone.

With mournful tidings often greeted,
   Until my soul was sick and sore,
My heart at last would not be cheated
   With what had cured its pains before.

So deep and bitter was my sorrow,
   Existence was a constant pain;
I wished not to perceive the morrow
   Or greet the gaze of man again.

Just then, when all was dark before me,
   And hope had closed her wing to die,
The music of a voice stole o'er me
   Scarce louder than an infant's sigh.

The words were few, but oh, how tender!
   Their hallowed accents still I hear;
They made my stubborn grief surrender,
   And banished every sinking fear.

Oh ye who have no goods, nor money,
   To give to those who mourn and weep,
Kind words are sweeter far than honey,
   And twice ten thousand times as cheap.

                   JULIAN CROMER.

THE BRIDEGROOM'S DOVE.

"O my Dove! in the clefts of the rock, in the secret of the stairs!" Cant. ii. 14.

"My Dove!" The Bridegroom speaks. To whom?
   Whom, think'st thou meaneth He?
Say, O my soul! canst thou presume
   He thus addresseth thee?
Yes, 'tis the Bridegroom's voice of love,
Calling thee, O my soul! His Dove!

The Dove is gentle, mild, and meek:
   Deserve I, then, the name?
I look within, in vain to seek
   Aught which can give a claim:
Yet, made so by redeeming love,
My soul, thou art the Bridegroom's Dove!

Methinks, my soul, that thou may'st see,
   In this endearing word,
Reasons why Jesus likens thee
   To this defenceless bird;
Reasons which show the Bridegroom's love
To His poor, helpless, timid Dove!

The Dove, of all the feathered tribe,
   Doth least of power possess:—
My soul, what better can describe
   Thine utter helplessness?
Yet courage take! the Bridegroom's love
Will keep, defend, protect His Dove!

The Dove hath neither claw nor sting,
  Nor weapon for the fight:
She owes her safety to her wing,
  Her victory to flight.
A shelter hath the Bridegroom's love
Provided for His helpless Dove!

The Hawk comes on in eager chase,—
  The Dove will not resist;
In flying to her hiding-place,
  Her safety doth consist.
The Bridegroom opes his arms of love,
And in them folds His panting Dove!

Nothing the Dove can now molest,
  Safe from the fowler's snare;
The Bridegroom's bosom is her nest—
  Nothing can harm her there.
Encircled by the arms of love,
Almighty power protects the Dove!

As the poor Dove, before the Hawk,
  Quick to her refuge flies,
So need I, in my daily walk,
  The wing which faith supplies
To bear me where the Bridegroom's love
Will place beyond all harm His Dove!

My soul, of native power bereft,
  To Calvary repairs;—

Immanuel is the *rocky cleft*
 The secret of the stairs!
Since placed *there* by the Bridegroom's love
What evil can befal His Dove!

Though Sinai's thunder round her roars,
 Though Ebal's lightnings flash,
Though Heaven a fiery torrent pours,
 And riven mountains crash—
Through all, the "still small voice" of love
Whispers, "Be not afraid, my Dove!"

What though the heavens away may pass,
 With fervent heat dissolve,
And round the sun, this earthly mass
 No longer shall revolve!
Behold a miracle of love!
The lion quakes, but not the Dove!

My soul, now hid within a rock,
 (The "Rock of Ages" called,)
Amid the universal shock
 Is fearless, unappalled;—
A cleft therein, prepared by love,
In safety hides the Bridegroom's Dove!

O happy Dove! thus weak, thus safe;
 Do I resemble her?
Then to my soul, O Lord! vouchsafe
 A dove-like character!
Pure, harmless, gentle, full of love
Make me in spirit, Lord, a Dove!

O Thou, who on the Bridegroom's head
  Did'st, as a Dove, come down,
Within my soul Thy graces shed,
  Establish there Thy throne.
There shed abroad a Saviour's love,
Thou, holy, pure, and heavenly Dove!
Anon.

DROPS OF HONEY.

Drops of Honey—let them fall
  From the lip, and from the pen;
Scatter them at sorrow's call:
  Stay not, asking where? or when?
Let them fall, these drops of honey;
  The poor need them, who've no money.

Drops of Honey—human bees
  Cluster round us, daily craving
Just one drop—one sweet hearts-ease;
  For him, who life's storm is braving;
Then let fall, these drops of honey,
  They may prize them, who have money.

Drops of Honey—kindly words,
  Haste to breathe them every hour;
Sweeter than the song of birds;
  Rich and poor both feel their power.
And all can give these drops of honey,
  Which some hearts value, more than money.
Mrs. Anger.

ONE BY ONE.

One by one, the sands are flowing,
    One by one the moments fall;
Some are coming, some are going,
    Do not strive to grasp them all.

One by one, thy duties meet thee,—
    Let thy whole strength go to each;
Let no future dreams elate thee,
    Learn thou first what these can teach.

One by one, bright gifts from Heaven,
    Joys are sent thee here below,
Take them readily when given,
    And as calmly let them go.

One by one, thy griefs shall meet thee:—
    Do not fear an armed band:
One will pass, as others greet thee,
    Shadows flitting through the land;

Do not look at Life's long sorrow,
    See how small each moment's pain;
God will, for thee, each to-morrow
    Every-day begin again.

Every hour that flits so slowly
    Has its task to do or bear;
Luminous the crown and holy,
    If thou set each gem with care.

Do not linger with regretting,
   Or for error's hour despond,
Nor, thy daily toil forgetting,
   Look too eagerly beyond.

Hours are golden links, God's token,
   Reaching Heaven one by one,
Take them, lest the chain be broken
   Ere the pilgrimage be done.
ADELAIDE A. PROCTOR.

"STREW ON LIFE'S PATH A FLOWER."

Oh strew on life's wild path a flower,
   Ye that have one to spare;
To cheer the pilgrim on his road,
   And lessen human care.

Some little gift we all may give,
   However poor or low;
To cheer a brother in distress,
   And mitigate his woe.

A kindly word will never make
   The giver sadly poor.
And know that even these are sweet
   To hearts that much endure!

Yea, many a kindly office we
  May for each other do;
That in the coming hours of time
  May prove refreshing dew!

Refreshing to our weary souls,
  When earthly things shall pass·
And all our lofty plans shall fall
  To dust, and break like glass!

If ye have gold enough to spare,
  Let not the widow sigh,
Amid her little orphan ones,
  But all her wants supply.

God with an overruling hand,
  Dispenses wealth to some;
Yet such are only stewards here,
  For earth is not our home.

Bind up the broken heart with love,
  And cheer each fainting one;
Yield kindness unto all who need:—
  This duty should be done.

It will repay thee sevenfold;
  Such gentle deeds shall be
Undying as thy deathless soul
  In bright eternity!

Anon.

HASTE NOT—REST NOT.

Without haste, and without rest—
Bind the motto to thy breast;
Heed not flowers that round thee bloom,
Bear it onward to the tomb.

Ponder well, and know the right;
Onward, then, with all thy might;
Haste not—years can ne'er atone
For one restless action done.

Duty be thy polar guide—
Do the right, whate'er betide.
Haste not—rest not—conflicts past,
God shall crown thy work at last.
From the German of Goethe.

HOPE EVER.

The night is mother of the day,
    The winter of the spring:
And ever upon old decay,
    The greenest mosses cling.
Behind the cloud the starlight lurks;
    Through showers the sunbeams fall;
For God, who loveth all his works,
    Has left his hope with all.
Anon.

GENTLE WORDS.

It is not much the world can give,
   With all its subtle art,
And gold and gems are not the things,
   To satisfy the heart.
But oh! if those who cluster round
   The altar and the hearth,
Have gentle words and loving smiles,
   How beautiful is earth!

Anon.

THE WEALTH OF KINDNESS.

Oh, leave a smile of kindness
   Wherever you may go!
It will ease the soul of sadness
   And dry the tears that flow;
The heart that's well nigh breaking
   Will feel its soothing power;
Then leave a look of kindness,
   It costs you nothing more.

We know not half the sorrow
   That bows our kinsman down,
Nor what is gained by giving,
   A kind look for a frown!
'Tis but a simple dowry
   Which wealth is far below!

Be kind, then, to the wretched,
   And thou shalt mercy know!

Is there a heart among us
   Without some secret chord,
That vibrates not from kindness—
   From just a simple word?—
Its rays are like the sunshine
   That parts the gathering gloom;
Then shed those beams of kindness!—
   They'll shine upon thy tomb!
Anon.

EXTRACTS.

We all might do good
   When we often do ill;
There is always the way
   If we have but the will.
Though it be but a word,
   Kindly breathed, or suppressed,
It may guard off some pain,
   Or give peace to some breast!
Anon.

Who blesses others in his daily deeds
Will find the healing that his spirit needs,
For every flower in other's pathway thrown
Confers its fragrant beauty on our own.
Anon.

Oh God of glory! thou hast treasured up
    For me my little portion of distress,
But with each draught, in every bitter cup
    Thy hand hath mixed, to make its sourness less,
Some cordial drop, for which thy name I bless.
Anon.

Let us draw their mantles o'er us,
    Which have fallen in our way;
Let us do the work before us,
    Cheerly, bravely, while we may;
Ere the long night silence cometh,
    And with us it is not day.
Anon.

KINDNESS.

  'Tis a little thing,
To give a cup of water, yet its draught
Of cool refreshment, drained by fever's lips,
May send a shock of pleasure to the soul
More exquisite than when nectarian juice
Renews the life of joy in happiest hours.
  'Tis a little thing to speak some common word
Of comfort, which hath almost lost its use;
Yet on the ear of him, who thought to die
Unmourned, 'twill fall like choicest music.
TALFOURD.

TEMPTATION.

How many forms it shows to us,
    How many shapes it wears!
With what bewitching gentleness
    It lays its many snares!
Oh! when the heart is light and free,
    All confidence and joy,
And we in sunshine careless sit,
    With nothing to alloy,

How stealthily it creeps around
    The portals of the mind!
The most unguarded, yielding point,
    Seeks eagerly to find.
To every grade its form it suits,
    To minds of every hue,
To every earthly being, comes,
    With semblance ever new.

It comes, to make us food for thought,
    For deep remorse and pain;
To make us wish the hours recalled,
    And wish, and wish in vain.
Oh, for a talisman! to ward
    This fair deceit away!
'Tis dangerous to admit it near;
    'Tis death with it to play.

Anon.

SINCERITY.

Very many are the blessings
    Cast around our pilgrim way
Kindly greetings, love's caressings,
    Cheer our hearts from day to day;
But of all the things we see,
    Loveliest is sincerity.

Men may look with smiles upon us,
    Help us forward on our way,
Give the grasp of seeming fondness,
    Chase the cares of life away;
But what kindness will it be,
    If it lack sincerity?

We would chant in glowing numbers,
    Words of love and deeds of fame,
But the eye that never slumbers,
    Might deny them e'en a name;
For His awful scrolls on high
    Are records of sincerity.

If we trust in Truth's direction,
    Though distresses sore assail,
We shall witness sure protection,
    While the hypocrites shall fail;
Let our earnest wishes be
    For thy gifts—Sincerity.

Very simple may the dressing
  Of our guileless spirits seem,
But if Jesus give his blessing
  They will glow with purest beam;
For each word and deed will be
  Shining with sincerity.

Heavenly Father! Truth immortal
  Is the herald of Thy throne—
And he opes its glittering portal
  To the upright heart alone;
For we cannot live with Thee
  If we lack sincerity.
                              Anon.

KINDNESS.

A LITTLE word in kindness spoken,
  A motion or a tear,
Has often healed the heart that's broken,
  And made a friend sincere.

A word—a look,—has crushed to earth
  Full many a budding flower;
Which, had a smile but owned its birth,
  Would bless life's darkest hour.

Then deem it not an idle thing,
  A pleasant word to speak;
The face you wear, the thoughts you bring,
  A heart may heal or break.
                              Anon.

THERE'S GOOD IN EVERY HEART.

Wouldst thou win the crime-stained wanderer back
From Vice's dark and hideous track?
Let not a frown thy brow deform,
'Twill add but fierceness to the storm.
Deal kindly. In that bosom dark,
Still lingers Virtue's glimmering spark.
Plead with him—'tis the nobler part—
There's something good in every heart.

Bring to his mind the early time
Ere sin had stained his soul with crime;
When fond affection blessed his hours,
And strewed his joyous path with flowers;
When sportive jest, and harmless glee,
Bespoke a spirit pure and free.
Plead with him—'tis the nobler part—
There's something good in every heart!

There was a time that heart did rest
Close to a mother's yearning breast—
A time his ear the precepts caught
A kind and virtuous father taught.
It matters not what treacherous ray
First lured his steps from Virtue's way;
Enough to know thou yet mayst save
That soul from sin's engulphing wave.
Plead with him—act the nobler part—
There's something good in every heart.

Anon.

IDOLS.

Whatever passes as a cloud between
The mental eye of faith, and things unseen,
Causing that bright world to disappear,
Or seem less lovely, and its hopes less dear;
This is our world, our idol, though it bear
Affection's impress, or devotion's air!

Anon.

THE CRICKET.

The cricket, he dwells in the cold, cold ground,
   At the foot of the old oak tree,
And all through the lengthened autumn night,
   A merry song sings he.
He whistles a clear and merry tune,
By the sober light of the silver moon.
     The winds may moan
     With a hollow tone
All through the leaves of the rustling tree;
     The clouds may fly
     Through the deep blue sky,
The flowers may droop, and the brooklet sigh,
     But never a fig cares he.
He whistles a clear and merry tune
By the sober light of the silver moon,
All through the lengthened autumn night,
     And never a fig cares he.

There's a tiny cricket within thy heart,
   And a pleasant song sings he;
He sings of the mercies and goodness of God
   That hourly fall upon thee.
Let him whistle loud and clear,
Never drown him in a tear;
There's darkness enough on earth, I trow,
Without the gloom of a gloomy brow;
Darkness enough in the home of the poor,
That never comes to thy lofty door.
   Forth with a smile,
    Their woe to beguile;
Forth to lighten the heavy gloom,
Forth to brighten the clouded home;
Cheer up the soul that is shrouded in night;
   Tell it in tones of love,
Of hope on earth, and a land all bright—
   The land of Life and Love.
    And never fret,
    That you cannot get
Just what you want while you travel here.
This is not your lasting sphere;
   Trials, vexations,
   Are but temptations;
Use them aright; and they'll help you along
   In the narrow road
   That leads to God.
Use them aright, and they'll help you along.
   Never fret,
   You'll conquer yet.

Then let him whistle loud and clear,
Never drown him in a tear,
But all through the length of trouble's night,
Let him sing his merry song.

HADASSAH.

CHRISTIAN CALMNESS DISTURBED.

We walked by the side of the tranquil stream
That the sun had tinged by his parting beam;
The water was still, and so crystal clear,
That every spray had its image there.

And every reed that o'er it bowed,
And the crimson streak, and the silver cloud;
And all that was bright, and all that was fair,
And all that was gay, was reflected there.

And they said it was like to the chastened breast
That religion soothes to a holy rest,
When sorrow has tamed the impassioned eye,
And the bosom reflects its expected sky.

But I took a stone that lay beside,
And I cast it far on the glassy tide;
And gone was the charm of the pictured scene,
And the sky so bright, and the landscape green.

6

And I bade them mark, how an idle word,
Too lightly said, and too deeply heard;
Or a harsh reproof, or a look unkind,
May spoil the peace of the heavenly mind.

Though sweet be the peace, and holy the calm,
And the heavenly beam be bright and warm,
The heart that it gilds is all as weak
As the wave that reflects the crimson streak.

You cannot impede the celestial ray
That lights the dawn of eternal day;
But so may you trouble the bosom it cheers,
'Twill cease to be true to the image it bears.

CAROLINE FRY.

KINDNESS.

As stars upon the tranquil sea
   In mimic glory shine,
So words of kindness in the heart
   Reflect the source divine;
Oh then be kind, whoe'er thou art,
   That breathest mortal breath,
And it shall brighten all thy life,
   And sweeten even death.

CARLOS L. STUART.

THE BELIEVER AND HIS ECHO.

Bel.—True faith, producing love to God and man,
    Say, Echo, is not this the gospel plan?
Echo—"The gospel plan."

Bel.—Must I my faith in Jesus constant show,
    By doing good to all, both friend and foe?
Echo—"Both friend and foe."

Bel.—But if a brother hate and treat me ill,
    Must I return him good, and love him still?
Echo—"Love him still."

Bel.—If he my failings watches to reveal,
    Must I his faults as carefully conceal?
Echo—"As carefully conceal."

Bel.—But if my name and character he tears,
    And cruel malice too, too plain appears,
    And when I sorrow and affliction know,
    He loves to add unto my cup of woe,—
    In this uncommon, this peculiar case,
    Sweet Echo, say, must I still love and bless?
Echo—"Still love and bless."

Bel.—Whatever usage ill, I may receive,
    Must I still patient be, and still forgive?
Echo—"Still patient be, and still forgive."

Bel.—Why, Echo, how is this? Thou art, sure, a dove;
    Thy voice will teach me nothing else but love?
Echo—"Nothing else but love."

Bel.—Amen; with all my heart, then, be it so;
    'Tis all delightful, just, and good, I know,
    And now to practice I'll directly go.
Echo—"Directly go."

Bel.—Things being thus, then let who will object,
    My gracious God me surely will protect!
Echo—"Surely will protect."

Bel.—Henceforth on him I'll roll my every care,
    And both my friend and foe embrace in prayer!
Echo—"Embrace in prayer."

Bel.—But after all these duties, when they're done,
    Must I in point of merit them disown,
    And trust my soul on Jesus's blood alone?
Echo.—"On Jesus's blood alone."

Bel.—Echo, enough! Thy counsel, to my ear
    Is sweeter than the dew-drop's tear;
    Thy wise instructive lessons please me well;
    Till next we meet again, farewell! farewell!
Echo—"Farewell! farewell!"

                                       Anon

"AM I MY BROTHER'S KEEPER?"

Must I my brother keep,
  And share his pain and toil?
And weep with those that weep,
  And smile with those that smile,
And act to each a brother's part,
And feel his sorrows in my heart?

Must I his burden bear,
  As though it were my own;
And do as I would care
  Should to myself be done;
And faithful to his int'rests prove,
And, as myself, my neighbour love?

Must I reprove his sin?
  Must I partake his grief,
And kindly enter in,
  And minister relief—
The naked clothe, the hungry feed,
And love him, not in word, but deed?

Then Jesus, at thy feet
  A student let me be;
And learn, as it is meet,
  My duty, Lord, of thee:
For thou didst come on mercy's plan,
And all thy life was love to man!

Oh make me as Thou art,
  Thy Spirit, Lord, bestow—
The kind and gentle heart
  That feels another's woe;
And thus I may be like my Head,
And in my Saviour's footsteps tread.

REV. DR. RAFFLES.

LITTLE CHILDREN.

Speak gently to the little child,
  So guileless and so free,
Who, with a trustful, loving heart,
  Puts confidence in thee.
Speak not the cold and careless thoughts
  Which time has taught thee well,
Nor breathe one word, whose bitter tone
  Distrust might seem to tell.

If on his brow there rests a cloud,
  However light it be,
Speak loving words, and let him feel
  He has a friend in thee.
And do not send him from thy side,
  Till on his face shall rest,
The joyous look, the sunny smile,
  That mark a happy breast.

Oh! teach him, *this* should be his aim,—
    To cheer the aching heart,
To strive, where thickest darkness reigns,
    Some radiance to impart;
To spread a peaceful, quiet calm,
    Where dwells the noise of strife,
Thus doing good, and blessing all,
    To spend the whole of life.

To love, with pure affection deep,
    All creatures, great and small,
And still a stronger love to bear
    For Him, who made them all.
Remember, 'tis no common task
    That thus to thee is given,
To rear a spirit fit to be
    The inhabitant of heaven.

MARIA ROSEAU.

THE RIGHT MUST WIN.

Oh! it is hard to work for God,
    To rise and take his part,
Upon this battle-field of earth,
    And not sometimes lose heart.

He hides himself so wondrously,
    As though there were no God;
He is least seen when all the powers
    Of ill are most abroad.

Or He deserts us at the hour
  The fight is almost lost;
And seems to leave us to ourselves
  Just when we need Him most.

Ill masters good: good seems to change
  To ill with greatest ease;
And, worst of all, the good with good
  Is at cross purposes.

It is not so, but so it looks;
  And we lose courage then;
And doubts will come, if God hath kept
  His promises to men.

Ah! God is other than we think;
  His ways are far above,
Far above reason's height, and reached
  Only by childlike love.

The look, the fashion of God's ways,
  Love's life-long study are;
She can be bold, and guess, and act,
  When reason would not dare.

She has a prudence of her own;
  Her step is firm and free;
Yet there is cautious science, too,
  In her simplicity.

Workman of God! oh, lose not heart,
  But learn what God is like;

And in the darkest battle-field,
   Thou shalt know where to strike.

Oh, blessed is he to whom is given,
   The instinct that can tell
That God is on the field, when He
   Is most invisible.

And blessed is he who can divine
   Where real right doth lie,
And dares to take the side that seems
   Wrong to man's blindfold eye!

Oh, learn to scorn the praise of men!
   Oh, learn to love with God!
For Jesus won the world through shame,
   And beckons thee his road.

God's glory is a wondrous thing,—
   Most strange in all its ways,
And, of all things on earth, least like
   What men agree to praise.

Muse on his justice, downcast soul!
   Muse and take better heart;
Back with thine angel to the field;
   Success shall crown thy part!

God's justice is a bed, where we
   Our anxious hearts may lay,
And, weary with ourselves, may sleep
   Our discontent away.
                 FREDERICK FABER.

PRAY FOR THOSE THOU LOVEST.

"Pray for those thou lovest—thou wilt never have any comfort of his friendship for whom thou dost not pray."

Yes, pray for those thou lovest—thou may'st vainly, idly seek
The fervid words of tenderness, by feeble words, to speak;
Go, kneel before thy Father's throne, and meekly, humbly there
Ask blessings for the loved one, in the silent hour of prayer.

Yes, pray for those thou lovest; if unaccounted wealth were thine,
The treasures of the boundless deep, the riches of the mine,
Thou could'st not to thy cherished friend so dear a gift impart
As the earnest benediction of a deeply loving heart.

Seek not the worldling's friendship, it shall droop and wane ere long,
In the cold and heartless glitter of the pleasure-loving throng;
But seek the friend who, when thy prayer for him shall murmured be,
Breathes forth, in faithful sympathy, a fervent prayer for thee.

And should thy flowery path of life become a path of pain,
The friendship formed in bonds like these, thy spirit shall sustain ;
Years may not chill, nor change invade, nor poverty impair,
The love that grew and flourished at the holy time of prayer.

Mrs. Addy.

CLOUD OR SUN.

He sendeth sun, he sendeth shower,
Alike they're needful to the flower;
And joys and tears alike are sent
To give the soul fit nourishment.
As comes to me or cloud or sun,
Father! thy will, not mine, be done.

Can loving children e'er reprove
With murmurs whom they trust and love?
Creator, I would ever be
A trusting, loving child to thee;
As comes to me or cloud or sun,
Father! thy will, not mine, be done.

Oh, ne'er will I at life repine :—
Enough that thou hast made it mine.

Where falls the shadow cold of death,
I yet will sing with parting breath—
As comes to me or shade or sun,
Father! thy will, not mine, be done.

Mrs. Sarah F. Adams.

SECRET GRIEF.

"The heart knoweth his own bitterness." Prov. xiv. 10.

A STRANGE power hath the human heart,
  By heaven in mercy given,
Strength to perform its wonted part,
  While silently 'tis riven;
To smile e'en while each tender string
  Is broken one by one;
Hope to the fainting breast to bring
  While in its own lives none.

To sit beside the sufferer's bed,
  And dry the falling tear,
To gently hold the sinking head,
  And chase away each fear;
To gaze upon the trembling form,
  Till the lone heart seems broken,
And yet amid the fearful storm
  To give of grief no token.

To hear that voice, whose slightest tone
    Has sweetest music been,
Grow weaker, fainter, till each moan
    The listening ear drinks in;
Yet still unmoved, with placid brow,
    To meet that languid eye,
Nor show the parting spirit now
    How gladly it would die.

To shut, within the blighted heart,
    The agony and strife,
And meekly bear our destined part
    Amid the scenes of life,
Nor cast around our own loved throng,
    The gloom that reigneth there;
To check the smile, the cheerful song,
    To cloud this world so fair.

But oh! the soul could never bear
    This weight of silent grief,
Did not its woe one bosom share,
    One kindly bring relief;
One who, to sympathize, to cheer,
    The path of sorrow trod;
One to suffering ever near;
    'Tis thine, O Son of God!

'Tis thine to bind the bleeding heart,
    To calm the troubled breast,
Strength, hope, and heavenly peace impart
    To give the weary rest;

To point beyond this world of pain,
 To that bright home above,
Where those who part may meet again,
 Joined in unfading love.

Mrs. Martha Canfield.

I AM WEARY.

I am weary of straying—oh fain would I rest
In the far-distant land of the pure and the blest,
Where sin can no longer her blandishments spread,
And tears and temptations for ever are fled.

I am weary of hoping, where hope is untrue,
As fair, but as fleeting, as morning's bright dew.
I long for that land whose blest promise alone
Is changeless and sure as eternity's throne.

I am weary of sighing o'er sorrows of earth,
O'er joy's gloomy visions, that fade at their birth—
O'er the pangs of the loved, which we cannot assuage,
O'er the blightings of youth, and the weakness of age.

I am weary of loving what passes away—
The sweetest, the dearest, alas! may not stay;
I long for that land where those partings are o'er,
And death and the tomb can divide hearts no more.

I am weary, my Saviour, of grieving thy love;
Oh, when shall I rest in thy presence above?
I am weary, but oh, never let me repine,
While thy word, and thy love, and thy promise are
    mine.

Anon.

OH! FOR THE HAPPY DAYS GONE BY.

Oh! for the happy days gone by,
  When love ran smooth and free,
Days when my spirit so enjoyed
  More than earth's liberty!

Oh! for the times when on my heart
  Long prayer had never palled,
Times when the ready thought of God
  Would come when it was called?

Then when I knelt to meditate,
  Sweet thoughts came o'er my soul,
Countless, and bright, and beautiful,
  Beyond my own control.

Oh! who hath locked those fountains up?
  Those visions who hath stayed?
What sudden act hath thus transformed
  My sunshine into shade?

This freezing heart, O Lord! this will
   Dry as the desert sand—
Good thoughts that will not come, bad thoughts
   That come without command—

A faith that seems not faith, a hope
   That cares not for its aim,—
A love that none the hotter grows
   At Jesus's blessed name.

The weariness of prayer, the mist
   O'er conscience overspread—
The chill repugnance to frequent
   The feast of angel's bread:

If this drear change be thine, O Lord!
   If it be Thy sweet will,
Spare not, but to the very brim
   The bitter chalice fill;

But if it hath been sin of mine,
   Oh! show that sin to me—
Not to get back the sweetness lost,
   But to make peace with Thee.

One thing, alone, dear Lord, I dread:
   To have a secret spot
That separates my soul from Thee,
   And yet to know it not.

Oh! when the tide of graces set
   So full upon my heart,

I know, dear Lord, how faithlessly
   I did my little part.

I know how well my heart hath earned
   A chastisement like this,
In trifling many a grace away
   In self-complacent bliss.

But if this weariness hath come
   A present from on high,
Teach me to find the hidden wealth
   That in its depths may lie;

So in this darkness I can learn
   To tremble and adore,
To sound my own vile nothingness,
   And thus to love Thee more;

To love Thee, and yet not to think
   That I can love so much;
To have Thee with me, Lord! all day
   Yet not to feel Thy touch.

If I have served Thee, Lord, for hire,
   Hire which Thy beauty showed;—
Ah! I can serve Thee now for nought
   And only as my God!

Oh! blessed be this darkness then,
   This deep in which I lie,
And blessed be all things that teach
   God's dread supremacy!

                  FREDERICK FABER.

THE WILL OF GOD.

I worship Thee, sweet will of God!
    And all thy ways adore,
And every day I live, I seem
    To love Thee more and more.

Thou wert the end, the blessed rule
    Of Jesus's toils and tears;
Thou wert the passion of his heart,
    Those three-and-thirty years.

And, he hath breathed into my soul,
    A special love of Thee,
A love to lose my will in his,
    And by that loss be free.

I love to see Thee bring to nought
    The plans of wily men;
When simple hearts outwit the wise,
    Oh thou art loveliest then!

The headstrong world, it presses hard
    Upon the church full oft;
And then how easily thou turn'st
    The hard ways into soft.

I love to kiss each print where thou
    Hast set thine unseen feet;
I cannot fear thee, blessed will!
    Thine empire is so sweet.

When obstacles and trials seem
    Like prison walls to be,
I do the little I can do,
    And leave the rest to thee.

I know not what it is to doubt;
    My heart is ever gay:
I run no risk, for, come what will,
    Thou always hast thy way.

I have no cares, oh blessed will!
    For all my cares are thine;
I live in triumph, Lord, for thou
    Hast made thy triumphs mine.

And when it seems no chance nor change
    From grief can set me free,
Hope finds its strength in helplessness,
    And gaily waits on thee.

Man's weakness, waiting upon God,
    Its end can never miss,
For men on earth no work can do
    More angel-like than this.

Ride on, ride on triumphantly,
    Thou glorious will! ride on;
Faith's pilgrim sons behind thee take
    The road that thou hast gone.

He always wins who sides with God,
    To him no chance is lost;

God's will is sweetest to him when
    It triumphs at his cost.

Ill that he blesses is our good,
    And unblest good is ill,
And all is right that seems most wrong,
    If it be his sweet will!

FREDERICK FABER.

USE ME.

MAKE use of me, my God!
    Let me not be forgot;
A broken vessel cast aside—
    One whom thou needest not.

I am thy creature, Lord,
    And made by hands divine;
And I am part, however mean,
    Of this great world of thine.

Thou usest all thy works—
    The weakest things that be;
Each has a service of its own,
    For all things wait on Thee.

Thou usest the high stars,
    The tiny drops of dew,

The giant peak, and little hill;
   My God, oh use me too!

Thou usest tree and flower,
   The rivers vast and small:
The eagle great, the little bird
   That sings upon the wall.

Thou usest the wide sea,
   The little hidden lake,
The pine upon the Alpine cliff,
   The lily in the brake.

The huge rock in the vale,
   The sand-grain by the sea,
The thunder of the rolling cloud,
   The murmur of the bee!

All things do serve Thee here—
   All creatures, great and small;
Make use of me, of me, my God,
   The weakest of them all.
                    HORATIUS BONAR.

NEARER HOME.

One sweetly solemn thought
   Comes to me o'er and o'er,—
I'm nearer home to-day
   Than I ever have been before.

Nearer my Father's house,
    Where the many mansions be,
Nearer the great white throne,
    Nearer the jasper sea.

Nearer the bound of life,
    Where we lay our burdens down,
Nearer leaving the cross,—
    Nearer wearing the crown.

But lying, darkly between,
    Winding down through the night,
To the dim and unknown stream,
    That leads me at last to the light.

Close, closer my steps
    Come to the dark abysm,
Closer, death to my lips
    Presses the awful chrysm.

Saviour, perfect my trust,
    Strengthen the might of my faith,
Let me feel as I would when I stand
    On the rock of the shore of death.

Feel as I would when my feet,
    Are slipping over the brink ;
For, it may be, I'm nearer home,—
    Nearer now than I think.

                                    CAREY.

YONDER.

No shadows yonder!
   All light and song;
Each day I wonder,
   And say how long
Shall time me sunder
   From that dear throng?

No weeping yonder!
   All fled away;
While here I wander
   Each weary day,
And sigh as I ponder,
   My long, long stay.

No partings yonder!
   Time and space never
Again shall sunder;
   Hearts cannot sever;
Dearer and fonder,
   Hands clasp for ever.

None wanting, yonder!
   Bought by the Lamb!
All gathered under
   The evergreen palm;
Loud as night's thunder
   Ascends the glad psalm.

HORATIUS BONAR.

DISTRACTIONS IN PRAYER.

Oh! dearest Lord, I cannot pray,
    My fancy is not free;
Unmannerly distractions come,
    And force my thoughts from thee.

The world, that looks so dull all day,
    Grows bright on me at prayer,
And plans that ask no thought but then,
    Wake up and meet me there.

All nature one full fountain seems
    Of dreamy sight and sound,
Which, when I kneel, breaks up its deep,
    And makes a deluge round.

Old voices murmur in my ear,
    New hopes start into life,
And past and future gaily blend
    In one bewitching strife.

My very flesh has restless fits;
    My changeful limbs conspire
With all these phantoms of the mind
    My inner self to tire.

I cannot pray; yet, Lord! thou knowest
    The pain it is to me
To have my vainly-struggling thoughts
    Thus torn away from thee.

Ah, Jesus! teach me how to prize
  These tedious hours when I,
Foolish and mute before thy face,
  In helpless worship lie.

Prayer was not meant for luxury,
  Or selfish pastime sweet;
It is the prostrate creature's place
  At his Creator's feet.

Had I kept stricter watch each hour,
  O'er tongue, and eye, and ear,
Had I but mortified all day
  Each joy as it came near,—

Had I, dear Lord! no pleasure found
  But in the thought of thee,
Prayer would have come unsought, and been
  A truer liberty.

Yet thou art oft most present, Lord!
  In weak distracted prayer;
A sinner out of heart with self,
  Most often finds thee there.

And prayer that humbles, sets the soul
  From all illusions free;
And teaches it how utterly,
  Dear Lord! it hangs on thee.

The soul, that on self-sacrifice
  Is covetously bent,

Will bless thy chastening hand that makes
   Its prayer its punishment.

Ah, Jesus! why should I complain?
   And why fear aught but sin?
Distractions are but outward things;
   Thy peace dwells far within!

These surface troubles come and go,
   Like rufflings of the sea;
The deeper depth is out of sight
   To all, my God, but Thee!
FREDERICK FABER.

IN THE FIELD.

Fighting the battle of Life!—
   With a weary heart and head;
For in the midst of the strife
   The banners of Joy are fled.

Fled and gone out of sight,
   When I thought they were so near:
And the music of Hope, this night,
   Is dying away on my ear.

Fighting the whole day long,
   With a very tired hand,—

With only my armour strong—
    The shelter in which I stand.

There is nothing left of *me*,—
    If all *my* strength were shown,
So small the amount would be,
    Its presence could scarce be known.

Fighting alone to-night,—
    With not even a stander-by,
To cheer me on in the fight,
    Or to hear me when I cry.

Only the Lord can hear,
    Only the Lord can see
The struggle within how dark and drear,
    Though quiet the outside be.

Fighting alone to-night
    With what a fainting heart!
Lord Jesus, in the fight
    Oh! stand not thou apart.

Body and mind have tried
    To make the field my own,
But when the Lord is on my side,
    He doth the work alone.

And when he hideth his face,
    And the battle-clouds prevail,
It is only through his grace
    If I do not utterly fail.

The word of old was true,
    And its truth shall never cease,—
"The Lord shall fight for you,
    And ye shall hold your peace."

Lord! I would fain be still
    And quiet behind my shield,
But make me to love thy will,
    For fear I should ever yield!

For when to destroy my foes,
    Thou lettest them strike at me,
And fillest my heart with woes,
    That joy may the purer be.

Even as now my hands,
    So doth my folded will,
Lie waiting thy commands,
    Without one anxious thrill.

But, as with sudden pain,
    My hands unclasp and fold,
So doth my will start up again,
    And take its old firm hold.

Lord, fix my eyes upon thee!
    And fill my heart with thy love,
And keep my soul till the shadows flee,
    And light breaks forth from above.

Anon.

WEARY!

My feet are worn and weary with the march
    Over the road, and up the steep hill-side;
Oh! City of our God, I fain would see
    Thy pastures green, where peaceful waters glide.

My hands are weary toiling, toiling on
    Day after day for perishable meat;
Oh! City of our God, I fain would rest—
    I sigh to gain thy glorious mercy-seat.

My garments, travel-worn, and stained with dust,
    Oft rent by briars, and thorns that crowd my way,
Would fain be made, O Lord, my righteousness,
    Spotless and white in heaven's unclouded day.

My heart is weary of its own deep sin,—
    Sinning, repenting, sinning still again;
When shall my soul thy glorious presence feel,
    And find, dear Saviour, it is free from stain?

Patience, poor soul! the Saviour's feet were worn;
    The Saviour's heart and hands were weary too,
His garments stained, and travel-worn, and old,
    His vision blinded with a pitying dew.

Love thou the path of sorrow that he trod;
    Toil on, and wait in patience for thy rest!
Oh! City of our God, we soon shall see
    Thy glorious walls,—home often loved and blest!

                              S. ROBERTS.

NOW THE CRUCIBLE IS BREAKING.

Now the crucible is breaking,
Faith its perfect seal is taking,
   Like the gold in furnace tried;
Through the test of sharp distresses
Those whom heaven most richly blesses,
   For its joys are purified.

Trial, when it weighs severely,
Stamps the Saviour's image clearly
   On the heart of all his friends;
In the frame his hands have moulded
Is a future life unfolded,
   Through the suffering which he sends.

Suffering curbs our wayward passions,
Childlike tempers in us fashions,
   And our will to his subdues:
Thus his hand, so soft and healing,
Each disordered power and feeling,
   By a blessed change renews.

Suffering keeps the thoughts compacted,
That the soul be not distracted
   By the world's beguiling art.
'Tis like some angelic warder,
Ever keeping sacred order
   In the chambers of the heart.

Suffering tunes the heart's emotion
To eternity's devotion;
   And awakes a fond desire
For the land where psalms are ringing
And with palms the martyrs singing,
   Sweetly to the harper's choir.

Suffering gives our faith assurance,
Makes us patient in endurance.
   Suffering! who is worth thy pains?
Here they call thee only torment—
There they call thee a preferment,
   Which not every one attains.

Brethren! grace which thus assuages
Suffering, is through diverse stages
   Reached by true disciples here;
While they're pierced by sharpest anguish,
While in many a death they languish,
   Watch through many a night of fear.

Though in health, with powers unwasted,
And with willing hearts we hasted
   To take up our Saviour's cross;
If through trial, our good Master
Should refine these powers the faster,
   What good Christian counts it loss?

In the depths of its distresses,
Each true heart the closer presses

To His heart with ardent love;
Ever longing, ever crying,
Oh! conform me to thy dying
   That I live with thee above!

Sighs and tears at last are over;
Breaking through its fleshy cover,
   Soars the soul to light away.
Who, while here below, can measure
That deep sea of heavenly pleasure,
   Spreading there, so bright for aye?

Day by day, O Jesus! nearer,
Show that bliss to me, and clearer,
   Till my latest hour I see.
Then, my weary striving ended,
May my spirit be attended,
   By bright angels, home to thee!

HARTMAN.

ALONE.

Alone! ah me, that word alone,
   How many a heart has breathed it low,
With tremulous despairing tone,
   And grief that none but God may know.

No eye may see the looming cloud,
   That settles dark o'er girlhood's morn,

Or view the cold and clammy shroud,
   Enfolding hopes so lately born.

And yet, perchance, a pall of dust
   And ashes o'er that form is spread;
Dear ones the heart had learned to trust,
   May now be with the dreamless dead.

The bark of life may seem to sail
   Upon a calm and waveless sea,
And lightly bound before the gale,
   Careering proudly, firm and free.

And yet that little bark may be
   The weary, 'biding place of grief—
Of brooding woe and misery
   That vainly seeks on earth relief.

Alas! how many bleeding chords
   Will tremble at the lightest touch,
And vibrate long to whispered words,
   Fearing and loving over-much.

Alone! that cold, harsh word, alone
   It chills the life-blood 'round the heart;
'Tis uttered with a wailing moan,
   When bitter, blinding tear-drops start.

Yet some are in the world alone,
   With countless millions thronging near,
No trusting heart to call their own,
   No voice to breathe sweet tones of cheer.

But oh! in Sorrow's darkest hour,
  "Our Father" every storm can calm,
The winds and waves obey his power,
  And He will pour a healing balm.

Upon the troubled, restless soul,
  If unto Him in faith we go;
Yielding our all to His control,
  He'll stay the rushing tide of woe.

Oh then, what though our course may lie
  Across an angry, rolling sea;
What though, at times our earthly sky,
  Obscured by threatening clouds may be.

What though in sorrow no fond tone
  Of human love should greet the ear;
We are not, cannot be *alone*,
  Our Father, God, is ever near.

SOPHRONIA.

THE PRAYER ANSWERED, THE REQUEST DENIED.

I THOUGHT 'twas Thine to give me, and I craved
One blessing more than all on earth beside;
I asked it often, and I asked it long,
It was not sin, and yet it was denied.

Didst Thou not hear the still repeated prayer?
Prayed I amiss, as if the due were mine?

Nor, simply resting on Thy love, exclaimed,
Fulfil Thy promise, Lord, for I am Thine.

Ah! foolish, He, who, from the ocean's depth,
Through roaring waters, heard the prophet's prayer,
Who marks the first faint breathing of desire
Can never deafen his paternal ear.

He heard me, yes, he listened, and he heard,
And held the blessing in his own right hand,
Whatever barred me from the good I sought
Had sunk to nothing at His sole command.

He heard, and might have granted, but he marked
The secret reservation of the soul,
The wish that almost to itself unknown,
Forbade the prayer that on the accents stole.

He marked the feeling that himself inspired,
He knew the heart he moulded, and he knew,
That while my lips the warm petition breathed,
I did not wish it, if he wished not too.

'Twas so, most Merciful! I did not say
I loved Thy will more than the thing I sought.
I asked an earthly good, but Thou perceiv'dst
Something was dearer, though I said it not.

Thou knewest I would not have it, might it mar
The better bliss to which my hopes aspire,
And mercy, yielding what thy wisdom knew,
Denied the prayer, to grant me the desire.

Anon.

NEVER MIND.

Soul, be strong, whate'er betide,
God himself is guard and guide—
With my Father at my side,
                Never mind!

Clouds and darkness hover near,
Men's hearts failing them for fear,
But be thou of right good cheer,
                Never mind!

Come what may, some work is done,
Praise the Father through the Son,
Goals are gained and prizes won,
                Never mind!

And if now the skies look black,
All the past behind my back,
Is a bright and blessed track;
                Never mind!

Stand in patient courage still,
Working out thy Master's will,
Compass good, and conquer ill;
                Never mind!

Fight, for all thy bullying boast,
Dark temptation's evil host,
This is thy predestined post,
                Never mind!

Be, then, tranquil as a dove;
Through these thunder-clouds above
Shines afar the heaven of love;
    Never mind!
   Martin Farquhar Tupper.

TRUST.

"My times are in thy hand."

Yet will I trust! in all my fears,
Thy mercy, gracious Lord, appears,
To guide me through this vale of tears,
    And be my strength.

Thy mercy guides my ebb and flow
Of health and joy, or pain and woe,
To wean my heart from all below,
    To Thee at length.

Yes! welcome pain which Thou hast sent,
Yes—farewell blessing Thou hast lent,
With Thee alone I rest content,
    For Thou art heaven.

My trust reposes safe and still,
On the wise goodness of Thy will,
Grateful for earthly good or ill,
    Which Thou hast given.

O blessed friend! O blissful thought!
With happiest consolation fraught—
Trust Thee I may, I will, I ought—
   To doubt were sin.
    MARTIN FARQUHAR TUPPER.

THE INNER CALM.

CALM me, my God, and keep me calm,
 While these hot breezes blow,
Be like the night-dew's cooling balm
 Upon earth's fevered brow.

Calm me, my God, and keep me calm,
 Soft resting on thy breast,
Soothe me with holy hymn and psalm,
 And bid my spirit rest.

Calm me, my God, and keep me calm;
 Let thine outstretching wing
Be like the shade of Elim's palm,
 Beside her desert spring.

Yes, keep me calm, though loud and rude
 The sounds my ear that greet;
Calm in the closet's solitude,
 Calm in the bustling street.

Calm in the hour of buoyant health,
 Calm in my hour of pain.

Calm in my poverty or wealth,
  Calm in my loss or gain.

Calm in the sufferance of wrong,
  Like Him who bore my shame,
Calm 'mid the threat'ning, taunting throng,
  Who hate Thy holy name.

Calm when the great world's news with power
  My listening spirit stir;
Let not the tidings of the hour
  E'er find too fond an ear.

Calm as the ray of sun or star
  Which storms assail in vain,
Moving, unruffled, through earth's war,
  The eternal calm to gain.

HORATIUS BONAR.

PROVIDENCE.

Just as a mother, with sweet pious face,
  Yearns towards her little children from her seat,
Gives one a kiss, another an embrace,
  Takes this upon her knee, that to her feet;
And while from actions, looks, complaints, pretences,
  She learns their feelings, and their various will,

To this a look, to that a word dispenses,
    And whether stern or smiling, loves them still;
So Providence, for us, high, infinite,
    Makes our necessities its watchful task,
Hearkens to all our prayers, helps all our wants,
    And e'en if it denies what seems our right,
Either denies because 'twould have us ask,
    Or seems but to deny, or in denying grants.

Anon.

CRAVING FOR REPOSE.

But to be still! oh, but to cease awhile
The panting breath, and hurrying steps of life,
The sights, the sounds, the struggle, and the strife
Of hourly being; the sharp, biting file
Of action, pelting on the tightened chain
Of rough existence; all that is not pain,
But rather weariness! oh! to be free,
But for a while from conscious entity!
To shut the banging doors and windows wide
Of restless sense, and let the soul abide,
Darkly, and stilly, for a little space,
Gathering its strength up to pursue the race;
Oh! but to rest a moment—but to rest
From this quick, gasping life, were to be blest!

FANNY KEMBLE.

THE IDLE LYRE.

There was an idle lyre
   'Mid heaven's choral band,
A messenger was summoned
   To hear his Lord's command—
That from among earth's children
   Some favoured one he'd bring,
Who had a skilful finger
   To sweep the golden string.

Oh! high and holy honour!
   Whose shall the glory be,
To make a music fitting
   The ear of Deity?
What mighty minstrel laurelled
   With wreaths which fame has given,
Shall now be counted worthy
   To join the ranks of heaven?

No master-mind, whose spirit
   Might lift itself to hymn
The praise of the Eternal
   With burning seraphim,—
Nor one whose life had lingered,
   Till age had quenched its fire,
Is from earth's myriads chosen
   To touch that silent lyre.

A little child was playing
   Beside his mother's knee,

Unconscious of the honour
    That was his destiny.
The angel bent above him,
    And breathed the low command,
And ere another morning
    The lyre was in his hand.

Ah! is the mother weeping,
    Because her baby boy
Is tasting purer pleasure
    And feeling holier joy,
Than she could ever yield him
    With her most soothing tone,
While yet the darling's bosom
    Was pillowed on her own?

We know that she will miss him—
    Unworn his garments lie,
And every way she turneth
    There's something meets her eye
That marks his painful absence,
    And from his vacant bed,
Like Rachel in her sorrow,
    She turns uncomforted.

Mourns she that he is taken
    Where every pain is o'er?
Where not a human passion
    Shall mar his quiet more?
Oh! could she hear the sweetness
    Of his angelic strain,

Not life's best gifts would tempt her
   To call him back again!

Though transient was his visit
   To this bleak world of ours,
The pleasant buds of promise
   Gave pledge of early flowers,
Whose perfect bloom we only
   Can see when it is given
To join, as kindred spirits,
   The choristry of heaven!
MARGARET JUNKIN.

THE ALPINE SHEEP.

AFTER our child's untroubled breath
   Up to the Father took its way,
And on our home the shade of death,
   Like a long twilight, haunting lay:

And friends came round, with us to weep
   Her little spirit's swift remove,
This story of the Alpine sheep
   Was told to us, by one we love:—

They in the valley's sheltering care,
   Soon crop the meadow's tender prime,

And when the sod grows brown and bare
   The shepherd strives to make them climb,

To airy shelves of pasture green
   That hang along the mountain's side,
Where grass and flowers together lean,
   And down through mist the sunbeams slide.

But nought can tempt the timid things
   That steep and rugged path to try,
Though sweet the shepherd calls and sings,
   And seared below the pastures lie :—

Till in his arms, their lambs he takes,
   Along the dizzy verge to go,
Then, heedless of the rifts and breaks,
   They follow on, o'er rock and snow.

And in those pastures lifted fair,
   More dewy soft than lowland mead,
The shepherd drops his tender care,
   And sheep and lambs together feed.

This parable, by nature breathed,
   Blew on me as the south wind free,
O'er frozen brooks that float unsheathed
   From icy thraldom to the sea.

A blissful vision, through the night
   Would all my happy senses sway,
Of the good Shepherd on the height
   Or climbing up the stony way,

Holding *our* little lamb asleep;
  And, like the burden of the sea,
Sounded that voice along the deep,
  Saying, "*Arise and follow me.*"

JAMES RUSSELL LOWELL.

INTO THE LIGHT.

I cry for peace, O God!
  My soul is dark as night,
I feel the chastening rod,
  But cannot see the light.
I know Thou art not far
  From every child of earth,
But sinful passions war
  Against the spirit's birth.

To calmer, holier life,
  Oh lend me of Thy strength,
That out of all this strife
  Peace may arise at length.
I fain would look to Thee,
  With never-faltering trust,
But Thou, O God, canst see
  How weak is this poor dust.

Thou knowest all my sin—
  Low at Thy feet I lie;

Help me to enter in
  To rest, before I die.
To cast this veil away,
  That I Thy love may see;
In deep distress I pray,
  O Father, pity me!

I am Thy child; through all
  This fearful, deepening night
I bend to hear Thy call—
  I wait to greet the light.
The morn will come; e'en now
  The midnight shadows flee;
With new-born hope I bow—
  My God, I trust in Thee.

Anon.

PRAYER FOR MERCY.

Throw away thy rod,
Throw away thy wrath!
  O my God,
Take the gentle path.

For my heart's desire
Unto thine is bent,
  I aspire
To a full consent.

Though I fail, I weep;
Though I halt in pace,
    Yet I creep
To the throne of grace.

Then let wrath remove;
Love will do the deed;
    For with love
Stony hearts will bleed.

Throw away thy rod;
Though man frailties hath,
    Thou art God,
Throw away thy wrath!

HERBERT.

BE YE PATIENT.

BESIDE the toilsome way
  Lowly and sad, by fruits and flowers unblest,
Which my worn feet treads sadly, day by day,
  Longing in vain for rest,—

An angel softly walks,
  With pale, sweet face, and eyes cast meekly down
The while, from withered flowers, and flowerless
    stalks
  She weaves my fitting crown.

A sweet and patient grace,
  A look of firm endurance, true and tried,

Of suffering meekly borne, rests on her face,
   So pure, so glorified.

And when my fainting heart
   Desponds and murmurs at the adverse fate,
Then quietly the angel's bright lips part—
   Murmuring softly—"Wait!"

"Patience," she softly saith,
   The Father's mercies never come too late;
Gird thee, and with patient strength and trusting
     faith
   And firm endurance wait.

Angels, behold, I wait!
   Wearing the thorny crown, through all life's
     hours,
Wait, till thy hand shall ope the eternal gate,
   And change the thorns to flowers.

Anon.

PRAISE FOR AFFLICTIONS.

For what shall I praise thee, my God, and my King,
For what blessings the tribute of gratitude bring?
Shall I praise thee for pleasure, for health, and for
    ease?
For the spring of delight, and the sunshine of peace?

Shall I praise thee for flowers that bloomed in my
  breast?
For joys in prospective, and pleasures possessed?
For the spirits that heightened my days of delight?
And the slumbers that sat on my pillow by night?

For this would I praise thee; but if only for this,
I should leave half untold the donation of bliss;
I thank thee for sickness, for sorrow, for care;
For the thorns I have gathered, the anguish I bear.

For nights of anxieties, watchings, and tears;
A present of pain, a prospective of fears;
I praise thee, I bless thee, my King and my God,
For the good and the evil thy hand hath bestowed.

The flowers were sweet, but their fragrance is flown,
They yielded no fruits, they are withered and gone;
The thorn, it was poignant, but precious to me;—
'Twas the message of mercy, it led me to Thee.
FRY.

THE SERVICE OF THE LORD.

"If any man serve me, let him follow me, and where I am,
there shall also my servant be."—John xii. 26.

How blessed from the bonds of sin,
  And earthly fetters free,
In singleness of heart and aim
  Thy servant, Lord, to be!

The hardest toil to undertake
  With joy at thy command;
The meanest office to receive,
  With meekness at thy hand.

With willing heart and longing eyes
  To watch before thy gate,
Ready to run the weary race,
  To bear the heavy weight;
No voice of thunder to expect
  But follow, calm and still,
For love can easily divine
  The One Beloved's will.

Thus may I serve thee, gracious Lord,
  Thus ever thine alone,
My soul and body give to thee,
  The purchase thou hast won;
Through evil, or through good report,
  Still keeping by thy side,
By life, or death, in this poor flesh,
  Let Christ be magnified.

How happily the working days
  In this dear service fly,
How rapidly the closing hour—
  The time of rest draws nigh!
When all the faithful gather home,
  A joyful company,
And ever where the Master is
  Shall his blest servants be.

SPITTA.

"CEASE THOU FROM MAN."

Cease thou from man—oh! what to thee
   Can thy poor fellow-mortals be?
Are they not erring, finite, frail?
   What can their utmost aid avail?

Their very love will prove a snare;
   Then, when thy heart becomes aware
Of its own danger, it will bleed
   For leaning on a broken reed.

Why does thy bliss so much depend
   On earthly relative or friend?
There is a Friend who changes never,
   The love He gives will last for ever.

He has withdrawn thee now, apart
   To teach these lessons to thy heart;
Has darkened all thy earthly scene
   That thou on Him alone may'st lean.

His precious love the balm supplies
   For which thy wounded spirit sighs;
That only medicine can make whole
   The weary, faint, and sin-sick soul.

Go to that Friend, poor aching heart,
   He knows how desolate thou art,
He waits, He longs to see thee blest,
   And in Himself to give thee rest.

Anon.

FATHER, I KNOW.

Father, I know that all my life
  Is portioned out by Thee,
And the changes that will surely come
  I do not fear to see.
But I ask Thee for a quiet mind,
  Intent on pleasing Thee.
I ask Thee for a thankful love
  Though constant watchings wise,
To meet the glad with cheerful smile,
  And to wipe the weeping eyes;
And a heart at leisure from itself
  To soothe and sympathize.
I would not have the restless will,
  That wanders to and fro
Seeking for some great thing to do
  Or secret thing to know.
I would be dealt with as a child,
  Led, guided where to go,
Wherever in the world I am,
  In whatsoe'er estate,
I have a fellowship with other hearts
  To keep and cultivate;
And a work of holy love to do,
  For the Lord on whom I wait.
I ask Thee for the daily strength,
  To none that ask denied,
And a mind to blend with outward life
  While keeping at Thy side.

Content to fill a little space
  So Thou be glorified!
And if some things I do not ask
  In my cup of blessing be,
I would have my spirit filled the more
  With gratitude to Thee.
More careful than to serve Thee much,
  To serve Thee perfectly.
There are thorns besetting every path,
  That call for patient care;
There is a crook in every lot,
  And a need for earnest prayer;
But a lowly heart that leans on Thee,
  Is happy everywhere.
In a service that Thy love appoints,
  There are no bonds for me;
For my secret heart is taught the truth,
  That makes thy children free;
And a life of self-renouncing love
  Is a life of liberty.
Mrs. Waring.

LIFE'S VOYAGER.

Voyager on life's troubled sea,
Sailing to eternity!
Turn from earthly things away—
Vain they are, and brief their stay;

Chaining down to earth the heart,
Nothing lasting they impart—
Voyager, what are they to thee?
Leave them all, and follow me!

Traveller on the road of life!
Seeking pleasure, finding strife—
Know the world can never give
Aught on which the soul can live;
Grasp not riches,—seek not fame—
Shining dust and sounding name!
Traveller, what are they to thee?
Leave them all, and follow me.

Pilgrim through this " vale of tears!"
Banish all thy doubts and fears;
Lift thine eyes,—a heaven's above!
Think,—there dwells a God of love!
Wouldst thou favour with him find?
Keep his counsels in thy mind!
Pilgrim! much He's done for thee!
Wilt thou, then, not follow me?

Wanderer from the Father's throne,
Hasten back—thy errings own:
Turn,—thy path leads not to heaven!
Turn,—thy faults will be forgiven!
Turn,—and let thy songs of praise
Mingle with angelic lays!
Wanderer, have they charms for thee?
I know they have—then follow me!

Anon.

POWER OF PRAYER.

There is an eye that never sleeps
   Beneath the wing of night,
There is an ear that never shuts
   When sinks the beam of light.

There is an arm that never tires
   When human strength gives way;
There is a love which never fails
   When earthly loves decay.

That eye is fixed on seraph throngs;
That ear is fixed on angels' songs;
That arm upholds the world on high;
That love is thrown beyond the sky.

But there's a power which man can wield,
   When mortal aid is vain;
That eye, that arm, that love to reach,
   That listening ear to gain;
That power is prayer, which soars on high,
And feeds on bliss beyond the sky.
Gems of English Poetry.

NOT HERE—NOT THERE.

This world, O God, like that above,
   Is bright to those who know Thy love;
Where'er they dwell, they dwell with Thee,
   In heaven, in earth, or in the sea.

To me remains nor place, nor time,
  My country is in every clime:
I can be calm, and free from care,
  On any shore, since God is there.

While place we seek, or place we shun,
  The soul finds happiness in none.
But with my God to guide my way,
  'Tis equal joy to go or stay.

Could I be cast where Thou art not,
  That were indeed a dreadful lot;—
But regions none, remote, I call
  Secure of finding God in all.
MADAME GUYON.

"THY WILL BE DONE."

My God, my Father, while I stray
Far from my home in life's rough way,
Oh teach me from my heart to say,
  "Thy will be done!"

Though dark my path, and sad my lot,
Let me be still, and murmur not,
But breathe the prayer, divinely taught,—
  "Thy will be done!"

What tho' in lonely grief I sigh,
For friends beloved, no longer nigh,
Submissive still would I reply,—
    "Thy will be done!"

If thou should'st call me to resign
What I most prize—it ne'er was mine;
I only yield Thee what was thine—
    "Thy will be done!"

Should pining sickness waste away
My life in premature decay,
My Father—still I strive to say,—
    "Thy will be done!"

If but my fainting heart be blest
With thy sweet Spirit for its guest,
My God, to thee I leave the rest—
    "Thy will be done!"

Renew my will from day to day,
Blend it with thine, and take away
All that now makes it hard to say,—
    "Thy will be done!"

Then when on earth I breathe no more
The prayer oft mixed with tears before,
I'll sing upon a happier shore,—
    "Thy will be done!"
                  CHARLOTTE ELLIOTT.

THE SOUL'S IMAGE.

What superscription, O my soul!
　　What image dost thou bear?
Do earth-stains mar its loveliness,
　　Is guilt reflected there?

What image dost thou wear, my soul,
　　Inwrought with life-long toil;
The heavenly bringing, precious hope,
　　Free from life's dust and soil?

Does holy love the impress leave,
　　Is charity within?
Is the soul's image bright and pure,
　　Or is it dimmed by sin?

Oh, I would bear thy image, Christ!
　　Engraved upon my soul;
With thee in pastures green would walk,
　　Until I reach the goal.

Anon.

AFFLICTION.

Count each affliction, whether light or grave,
God's messenger, sent down to thee. Do thou,
With courtesy, receive him; rise and bow,
And, ere his shadow cross thy threshold, crave
Permission first his heavenly feet to lave.

There lay before him all thou hast. Allow
No cloud of passion to usurp thy brow,
Or mar thy hospitality, no wave
Of mortal tumult to obliterate
The soul's marmoreal calmness. Grief should be
Like joy, majestic, equable, sedate,
Confirming, cheering, raising, making free,
Strong to consume small troubles, to commend
Great thoughts, grave thoughts, thoughts lasting
    to the end.

Anon.

COME TO ME.

Come to me, Lord, when first I wake,
As the faint lights of morning break;
Bid purest thoughts within me rise,
Like crystal dew-drops to the skies!

Come to me, in the sultry noon,
Or earth's low communings will soon,
Of Thy dear face, eclipse the light,
And change my fairest day to night.

Come to me in the evening shade,
And if my heart from Thee have strayed,
Oh, bring it back, and from afar,
Smile on me like Thine evening star.

Come to me in the midnight hour,
When sleep withholds its balmy power,
Let my lone spirit find its rest
Like John, upon my Saviour's breast.

Come to me through life's varied way;
And when its pulses cease to play
Then, Saviour, bid me come to Thee,
That where Thou art, Thy child may be!
Anon.

COMMON BLESSINGS.

LOVING word and kindly deed,
And that grace which doth exceed
Every other, though it bear
Not so high a name and air:—
Love's forbearance, daily seen
In the sweet and patient mien;
Household love, which vainly tries
To hide itself in new disguise:—
With all sympathies, which bind
Heart to heart, and mind to mind;—
Common blessings these appear,
But most excellent and dear:—
Health to gladden every day;
Hope to banish care away;
Love, prosperity to bless;
Prayer to sanctify distress;

Common blessings these may be,
But most precious unto me;
Treasures of our common lot
Not unnoticed or forgot,
Silent as ye come and go,—
Grateful hearts your presence know;—
Long continued may you be,
Common blessings, unto me.

Anon.

PROVIDENCE.

Look and listen, look and listen!
　Thou the guiding hand shalt see,
And a voice divinely tender
　Lovingly shall talk with thee.

Cling thou to that hand confiding,
　Even as a little child;
They who trust the heavenly guiding,
　Safely pass through deserts wild.

Safe through forests, lone and fearful,
　Safe through throngs where pleasures lure,
Safe alike in sunshine cheerful,
　And when clouds the way obscure.

Holding fast the hand so tender,
　Listening to the kindly voice,

Every fear thou may'st surrender
   And for evermore rejoice.

I could tell to thee a story—
   Many such there might be told—
Of a man, now old and hoary,
   Who, thus trusting, has grown old.

Through the storms of many winters
   That have gloomed above his head,
Through the colder storms of sorrow
   He in safety has been led.

Subject to the world's mutations,
   Oft in darkness, oft in fear,
Oft in dangers and temptations,
   Still the kindly voice was near,

Whispering to him, "Be not fearful,
   Thou shalt never go astray;
Let thy heart be brave and cheerful,
   I will lead thee on thy way."

What though foes would have bereft him
   Of his honourable name;
Seeking on that brow so noble
   To affix the brand of Shame.

What though early friends departed
   From before his lingering eye,
And full often, weary-hearted,
   Longed he far from earth to fly.

What though want, her terrors wearing,
  What though sickness crossed his way,
And the tempter, grown more daring,
  Dogged his footsteps day by day.

Yet in safety passed he onward,
  Passing toward the better land;
Listening to the voice so tender,
  Holding fast the guiding hand.

And the shadows lengthen round him,
  Yet he passes onward still;.
Heeding not the coming darkness,
  Feeling not the evening's chill.

Look and listen, look and listen,—
  Thou the guiding hand shalt see,
And a voice divinely tender,
  Lovingly shall talk with *thee!*

Anon.

HE LEADETH ME BESIDE STILL WATERS.

"He leadeth me!" O blessed thought!
O words with heavenly comfort fraught!
Whate'er I do, where'er I be,
Still 'tis God's hand that leadeth me!
  He leadeth me! He leadeth me!
  By his own hand he leadeth me.

Sometimes 'mid scenes of deepest gloom,
Sometimes where Eden's bowers bloom;
By waters still o'er troubled sea—
Still 'tis his hand that leadeth me!
  He leadeth me! He leadeth me!
  By his own hand he leadeth me.

Lord, I would clasp my hand in thine,
Nor ever murmur nor repine—
Content, whatever lot I see,
Since 'tis my God that leadeth me;
  He leadeth me! He leadeth me!
  By his own hand he leadeth me.

And when my task on earth is done,
When by thy grace the victory's won;
E'en death's cold wave I will not flee,
Since God through Jordan leadeth me.
  He leadeth me! He leadeth me!
  By his own hand he leadeth me.

Anon.

BRING ME HOME.

I know not the way I am going,
  But well do I know my guide;
With a child-like trust I give my hand
  To the mighty Friend by my side.
The only thing that I say to Him,
  As he takes it, is, "Hold it fast!

Suffer me not to lose my way
   But bring me home at last!"

As when some helpless wanderer,
   Alone, in an unknown land,
Tells the guide his destined place of rest,
   And leaves all else in his hand;—
'Tis home, 'tis home, that we wish to reach,
   He who guides us may choose the way,
Little we heed the path we take,
   If nearer home each day!
Anon.

THE GUESTS.

"Behold, I stand at the door and knock; if any man hear my voice, and open the door, I will come into him, and will sup with him, and he with me."—Rev. iii. 20.

SPEECHLESS Sorrow sat with me;
I was sighing wearily.
Lamp and fire were out; the rain
Wildly beat the window pane.
In the dark we heard a knock,
And a hand was on the lock;
One in waiting spake to me,
   Saying sweetly,
"I am come to sup with thee!"

All my room was dark and damp;
"Sorrow," said I, "trim the lamp;

Light the fire, and cheer thy face;
Set the guest-chair in its place."
And again I heard the knock;
In the dark I found the lock—
"Enter, I have turned the key!
  Enter, stranger,
Who art come to sup with me!"

Opening wide the door, he came;
But I could not speak his name;
In the guest-chair took his place,
But I could not see his face;
When my cheerful eye was beaming,
When my little lamp was gleaming,
And the feast was spread for thee,
  Lo! my Master
Was the guest that supped with me!
HARRIET McEWEN KIMBALL.

THINE.

THOU knowest my weakness, Lord, my every failing,
  Thoughts unexpressed;
Those sinful thoughts, my better ones assailing,
  That throng my breast.

More than I think my wicked heart contains,
  Thou canst divine;
Lord, at thy feet, thy love that heart detains;
  For I am thine.

Thou art my Master; may thy arms of love
    Around me twine,
And raise me to that blessed land above:
    Lord, I am thine.

Save me, that never more from out thy fold
    I go astray,
Within thy arms my feeble spirit hold;
    Turn not away.

Pardon, dear Lord, all that has been amiss,
    That grieves thee so;
Grant me a foretaste of that heavenly bliss
    I long to know.

Thy seal is on my brow; may a sweet calm
    And hope be mine;
That I may sing with joy this gracious psalm,
    Lord, I am thine.

Anon.

TARRY WITH ME.

TARRY with me, O my Saviour!
    For the day is passing by;
See! the shades of evening gather,
    And the night is drawing nigh!
Tarry with me! tarry with me!
    Pass me not unheeded by!

Many friends were gathered round me,
  In the bright days of the past;
But the grave has closed above them,
  And I linger here the last!
I am lonely; tarry with me
  Till the dreary night is past.

Dimmed for me is earthly beauty;
  Yet the spirit's eye would fain
Rest upon thy lovely features:
  Shall I seek, dear Lord, in vain?
Tarry with me, O my Saviour,
  Let me see thy smile again!

Dull my ear to earth-born music:
  Speak, thou Lord, in words of cheer:
Feeble, tottering, my footstep,
  Sinks my heart with sudden fear;
Cast thine arms, dear Lord, around me
  Let me feel thy presence near.

Faithful memory paints before me
  Every deed and thought of sin;
Open, thou, the blood-filled Fountain,
  Cleanse my guilty soul within:
Tarry thou, forgiving Saviour!
  Wash me wholly from my sin!

Deeper, deeper grow the shadows,
  Paler, now, the glowing West;

Swift the night of death advances;
   Shall it be the night of rest?
Tarry with me, O my Saviour!
   Lay my head upon thy breast!

Feeble, trembling, fainting, dying,
   Lord, I cast myself on thee:
Tarry with me, through the darkness!
   While I sleep, still watch by me,
Till the morning, then awake me;
   Dearest Lord, to dwell with thee.

Anon.

THY WAY, NOT MINE.

Thy way, not mine, O Lord,
   However dark it be;
Lead me by thine own hand,
   Choose out the path for me.

Smooth let it be, or rough,
   It will be still the best;
Winding or straight, it matters not;
   It leads me to thy rest.

I dare not choose my lot;
   I would not, if I might:
Choose thou for me, my God,
   So shall I walk aright.

The kingdom that I seek
    Is thine: so let the way
That leads to it be thine,
    Else I must surely stray.

Choose thou for me my friends,
    My sickness or my health;
Choose thou my cares for me,
    My poverty or wealth.

Not mine, not mine the choice
    In things or great or small;
Be thou my Guide, my Strength,
    My Wisdom, and my All.
HORATIUS BONAR.

"I HOLD STILL."

PAIN's furnace heat within me quivers,
    God's breath upon the flame doth blow,
And all my heart in anguish shivers,
    And trembles at the fiery glow:
And yet I whisper, as God will!
And in its hottest fire hold still.

He comes and lays my heart, all heated,
    On the hard anvil, minded so
Into his own fair shape to beat it
    With his great hammer, blow on blow,
And yet I whisper, as God will!
And at his heaviest blows hold still.

He takes my softened heart and beats it;
    The sparks fly off at every blow;
He turns it o'er and o'er and heats it,
    And lets it cool, and makes it glow:
And yet I whisper, as God will!
And in his mighty hand hold still.

Why should I murmur? for the sorrow
    Thus only longer-lived would be;
Its end may come, and will to-morrow,
    When God has done his work in me:
So I say, trusting, as God will!
And trusting to the end, hold still.

He kindles for my profit, purely,
    Affliction's glowing, fiery brand,
And all his heaviest blows are surely
    Inflicted by a Master-hand:
So I say, praying, as God will!
And hope in him and suffer still.
               From the German of Sturm.

BEARING THE CROSS.

THE heavier cross, the nearer heaven;
    No cross without, no God within.
Death, judgment, from the heart are driven,
    Amidst the world's false glare and din.
Oh! happy he, with all his loss,
Whom God hath set beneath the cross.

The heavier cross, the better Christian,—
　　This is the touchstone God applies;
How many a garden would lie wasting,
　　Unwet by showers from weeping eyes!
The gold by fire is purified;
The Christian is by trouble tried.

The heavier cross, the stronger faith;
　　The loaded palm strikes deeper root;
The vine-juice sweetly issueth
　　When men have pressed the clustered fruit.
And courage grows where dangers come,
Like pearls beneath the salt-sea foam.

The heavier cross, the heartier prayer;
　　The bruised herbs most fragrant are.
If wind and sky were always fair
　　The sailor would not watch the star;
And David's psalms had ne'er been sung,
If grief his heart had never wrung.

The heavier cross, the more aspiring;
　　From vales we climb to mountain crest;
The pilgrim of the desert tiring,
　　Longs for the Canaan of his rest.
The dove has here no rest in sight,
And to the ark she wings her flight.

The heavier cross, the easier dying;
　　Death is a friendlier face to see;
To life's decay one bids defying—
　　From life's distress one then is free.

The cross sublimely lifts our faith
To him who triumphed over death.

Thou Crucified! The cross I carry—
   The longer may it dearer be;
And, lest I faint whilst here I tarry,
   Implant thou such a heart in me,
That faith, hope, love, may flourish there,
Till for my cross the crown I wear.
                   From the German of Schmolk.

ONE HOUR WITH THEE.

One hour with thee, my God, when daylight breaks
   Over a world thy guardian care hath kept;
When the pleased soul from soothing slumber wakes,
   To praise the love that watched me while I slept;
When with new strength my pulse is beating free,
   My first, best, sweetest thoughts I'll give to thee.

One hour with thee, when busy day begins
   Its never-ceasing round of cumb'ring care;
When I must meet with toil, and pain, and sins,
   And through them all my cross must bear;
Oh then to arm me for the fight, to be
   Faithful to death, I'll spend one hour with thee.

One hour with thee, when rides the glorious sun
   High in mid heaven—when parting nature feels
Lifeless and overpowered, and man has done,
   For one short hour, with urging life's swift wheels,

In that deep pause, my soul from care shall flee,
  To make that hour of rest an hour with thee.

One hour with thee, when sadd'ning twilight flings
  Her soothing charm o'er lawn, and vale, and grove,
And there breathes up from all created things
  The sweet enthralling sense of thy dear love;
Then, when its influence descends on me,
  Oh then, my God, I'll spend an hour with thee!

One hour with thee, my God, when softly night
  Climbs the high heaven with solemn step and slow,
And thy sweet stars, unutterably bright,
  Are sending forth thy praise to all below;
Then, when my thoughts from earth to heaven would flee,
  Oh then, my God, I'll spend an hour with thee!
                                            Anon.

MINISTERING ANGELS.

Time and Patience! these are angels
  By our heavenly Father sent;
Whispering to our restless spirits
  "Cease to murmur, be content;
God, who is our truest friend
  Doth us aid in trials send.

When thy weary spirit faileth,
  'Neath the weary cross it bears,
God is not unmindful of thee—
  He is listening to thy prayers,
From his children's tearful pleading
  He will never turn unheeding.

Heart of mine! trust thou these angels!
  Lean on Patience, and be calm;
Trust in Time, who is preparing
  For thy grief a spirit balm.
God is merciful, and he
  Gave them charge concerning thee.

Anon.

COMMUNION WITH GOD.

Lord, I am come alone with Thee!
Thy voice to hear, Thy face to see,
  And feel Thy presence near;
It is not fancy's lovely dream,
Though wondrous e'en to faith it seem,
  That Thou dost wait me here.

A moment from this outward life,
Its service, self-denial, strife,
  I joyfully retreat;
My soul, through intercourse with Thee,
Strengthen'd, refresh'd, and calm'd should be,
  Its scenes again to meet.

How can it be that one so mean,
A sinner, selfish, dark, unclean,
  Thus in the Holiest stands?
And in that light divinely pure,
Which may no stain of sin endure,
  Lifts up rejoicing hands!

Jesus! the answer Thou hast given!
Thy death, Thy life, have opened heaven
  And all its joys to me;
Washed in thy blood—O wondrous grace!
I'm holy as the Holy Place
  In which I worship Thee.

How sweet, how solemn thus to lie
And feel Jehovah's searching eye
  On me well pleased can rest!
Because with his Beloved Son,
The Father's grace has made me *one*,
  I must be always blest.

The secret pangs I could not tell
To dearest friends—*Thou* knowest well;
  They claim Thy gracious heart;
Thou dost remove with tender care,
Or sweetly give me strength to bear
  The sanctifying smart.

Thy presence has a wondrous power!
The sharpest thorn becomes a flower,
  And breathes a sweet perfume;

Whate'er looked dark and sad before,
With happy light shines silvered o'er—
  There's no such thing as gloom!

Thou know'st I have a cross to bear;
The needful stroke Thou dost not spare,
  To keep me near Thy side;
But when I see the chastening rod
In Thy pierced hand, my Lord, my God,
  My soul is satisfied.

Anon.

CLING TO THE CRUCIFIED.

CLING to the Crucified!
His death is life to thee,—
Life for eternity.
His pains thy pardon seal;
His stripes thy bruises heal;
His cross proclaims thy peace,—
Bids every sorrow cease.
His blood is *all* to thee,
It purges thee from sin;
It sets thy spirit free—
It keeps thy conscience clean.
Cling to the Crucified!

HORATIUS BONAR.

THE HOUR OF PRAYER.

My God! is any hour so sweet,
From blush of morn to evening star,
As that which calls me to thy feet,
    The hour of prayer?

Blest is that tranquil hour of morn,
And blest that hour of solemn eve,
When on the wings of prayer upborne,
    The world I leave!

For then a day-spring shines on me,
Brighter than morn's ethereal glow;
And richer dews descend from thee,
    Than earth can know.

Then is my strength by thee renewed;
Then are my sins by thee forgiven;
Then dost thou cheer my solitude
    With hope of heaven.

No words can tell what sweet relief
There for my every want I find,
What strength for warfare, balm for grief,
    What peace of mind.

Hushed is each doubt, gone every fear;
My spirit seems in heaven to stay;
And e'en the penitential tear
    Is wiped away.

Lord! till I reach you blissful shore,
No privilege so dear shall be,
As thus, my inmost soul to pour
      In prayer to Thee.

CHARLOTTE ELLIOTT.

AT HOME IN HEAVEN.

Here in the body pent,
  Absent from Him I roam,
Yet nightly pitch my morning tent
  A day's march nearer home.

My Father's house on high,
  Home of my soul; how near
At times to Faith's foreseeing eye
  The golden gates appear!

Ah! then my spirit faints
  To reach the land I love,
The bright inheritance of saints,
  Jerusalem above.

Yet clouds will intervene,
  And all my prospect flies
Like Noah's dove, I flit between
  Rough seas and stormy skies.

Anon the clouds disperse,
  The winds and waters cease,
While sweetly o'er my gladdened heart
  Expands the bow of peace.

JAMES MONTGOMERY.

WAIT.

Be patient—life is very brief;
  It passes quickly by.
And, if it prove a troubled scene
  Beneath a stormy sky,
It is but like a shaded night
That brings a morn of radiance bright.

Be hopeful—cheerful faith will bring
  A living joy to thee;
And make thy life a hymn of praise,
  From doubt and murmur free:
While, like the sunbeam, thou wilt bless
And bring to others happiness.

Be earnest—an immortal soul
  Should be a worker true;
Employ thy talents for thy God,
  And ever keep in view
The judgment scene, the last great day
When heaven and earth shall pass away.

Be holy—let not sin's dark stain
    Thy spirit's whiteness dim;
Keep close to Jesus 'mid the world
    And trust alone in Him.
So 'midst thy business and thy rest,
Thou shalt be comforted and blest.

Be prayerful—ask, and thou shalt have
    Strength equal to thy day;
Prayer clasps the hand that guides the world;
    Oh make it then thy stay!
Ask largely, and thy God will be
A kingly giver unto thee.

Be ready—many fall around,
    Our loved ones disappear;
We know not when our call may come,
    Nor should we wait in fear;
If ready, we may calmly rest,
Living, or dying, we are blest.

Anon.

THE SOUL WAITING.

I am foot-sore and very weary,
    But I travel to meet a friend;
The way is long and dreary,
    But I know that it soon must end.

He is travelling fast, like the whirlwind,
   And though I creep slowly on,
We are drawing nearer, nearer,
   And the journey is almost done.

Through the heat of many summers,
   Through many a spring-time rain,
Through long autumns and weary winters,
   I have hoped to meet him, in vain.

On the day of my birth he plighted
   His kingly word to me;
I have seen him in dreams so often
   That I know what his smile must be.

I have toiled through the sunny woodland,
   Through fields that basked in the light,
And through the lone paths in the forest,
   I crept in the dead of night.

I will not fear at his coming,
   Although I must meet him alone;
He will look in my eyes so gently,
   And take my hand in his own.

Like a dream all my toil will vanish
   When I lay my head on his breast;
But the journey is very weary,
   And he only can give me rest!

                    ADELAIDE A. PROCTOR.

PILGRIM'S WAY-SONG.

I'm bound to the house of my Father;
    Oh, draw not my feet from the way,
Nor stop me, these wild flowers to gather;
    They droop at my touch, and decay!
I think of the flowers that are blooming
    In beauty unfading above,
The wings of kind angels perfuming,
    Who fly down on errands of love.

Of earth's shallow waters the drinking
    Is powerless my thirst to allay;
Their taste is of tears, while we're sinking
    Beside them where quicksands betray.
I long for the fount ever living,
    That flows by my Father's own door,
With waters so sweet and life-giving,
    To drink and to thirst never more.

The gold of this bright, happy dwelling,
    Makes all lower gold to look dim;
Its treasures, all treasures excelling,
    Shine forth, and allure me to Him.
The gems of this world I am treading
    In dust, where, as pebbles they lie;
To win the rich pearl that is shedding
    Its lustre so pure from on high.

For pains a torn spirit is feeling,
    No balsam from earth it receives,

I go to the tree that is healing,
　To drop in my wounds from its leaves.
A child that is weary with roaming,
　Returning in gladness to see
Its home, and its parent, I'm coming,—
　My Father, I hasten to thee!

HANNAH F. GOULD.

THE COURSE OF LIFE.
From a Spanish Poem.

OH, let the soul its slumber break,
Arouse its senses and awake,
　　To see how soon
Life with its glories glides away,
And the stern footstep of decay.
　　Comes stealing on:

How pleasure, like the passing wind,
Blows by, and leaves us naught behind
　　But grief at last;
How still our present happiness
Seems, to the wayward fancy, less
　　Than what is past.

Our lives, like hasting streams must be,
That into one engulphing sea
　　Are doomed to fall—
The sea of Death whose waves roll on,
O'er king and kingdom, crown and throne,
　　And swallow all.

Alike the river's lordly tide,
Alike the humble streamlets glide
    To that sad wave;
Death levels poverty and pride,
And rich and poor sleep side by side
    Within the grave.

Our birth is but the starting-place,
Life is the running of a race,
    And death the goal.
Then all our steps at last are brought,
That path alone, of all unsought,
    Is found of all.

To Thee, O God, my thoughts arise,
Thou great, eternal, good, and wise,
    To Thee I cry;
Gird me the race of life to run;
And give me then the victor's crown
    With Thee on high.

"He knoweth our frame—He remembereth that we are dust."

THEN, oh have pity, Father, on thy child,
Trembling alone, beneath the tempest wild,
My fragile bark tossed on life's dangerous sea,
Father, supreme! I raise my cry to Thee.

Thou to the restless waves can whisper peace,
And bid the storm its dark destruction cease,

Oh speak the word, Thou seest me struggling low,
In agony which only Thou canst know.

And only Thou canst save: oh let me share,
Father, once more thy kind and gracious care;
Though I have erred and wandered far from Thee,
Forgive, most Merciful, and set my spirit free.

Thou knowest how bitter is the strife within,
The ceaseless warring with unconquered sin,
Hovering 'twixt good and ill; oh let my soul
Soar far above the world and sin's control.

FANNIE RAYMOND.

WHISPERS OF THE GLORIFIED SPIRIT.

In youth I died, in maiden bloom;
   With gentle hand Death touched my cheek,
And with his touch there came to me
   A Spirit calm and meek.

He took from me all wish to stay;
   He was so kind, I feared him not:
My friends beheld my slow decline,
   And mourned my timeless lot.

They saw but sorrow; I descried
   The bliss that never fades away:
They felt the shadow of the tomb:—
   I marked the heavenly day.

I heard them sob, as through the night
    They kept their watch; then on my ear
Amid the sobbing fell a voice
    Their anguish could not hear.

"Come, and fear not," it softly cried;
    "We wait to lead thee to thy home."
Then leaped my spirit to reply,
    I come, I long to come.

I heard them whisper o'er my bed—
    Another hour, and she must die.
I was too weak to answer them,
    That endless life was nigh.

Another hour, with bitter tears,
    They mourned me as untimely dead;
And heard not how I sang a song
    Of triumph o'er their head.

They bore me to the grave, and thought
    How narrow was my resting-place;
My soul was roving high and wide
    At will through boundless space.

They clothed themselves in robes of black;
    Through the sad aisles the requiem rang;
Meanwhile the white-robed choirs of heaven
    A holy pæan sang.

Oft from my paradise I come,
    To visit those I love on earth,

I enter, unperceived, the door;
   They sit around the hearth.

And talk in saddened tone of me
   As one that never may return.
How little think they that I stand
   Among them as they mourn!

But time will ease their grief, and death
   Will purge their darkness from their eyes.
Then shall they triumph when they learn
   Heaven's solemn mysteries.
Anon.

"BE YE THANKFUL."

Col. iii. 15.

Oh be ye thankful, while ye breathe
   This wondrous vital air,
And pitch your tent upon the earth
   That God hath made so fair;
And rest upon the glorious hope
   A heavenly home to share.

Oh be ye thankful for the love
   Like dew around you shed,
That when you slumber, sets a watch
   Of angels round the bed;
And when you wake, with constant care
   Doth in your pathway tread.

Lord, make us thankful, for too oft,
  By fleeting sorrows bowed,
In the dark pall of discontent
  Our ingrate souls we shroud:
Lend us thy sunbeam, till we reach
  The sky without a cloud.
Anon.

HEAVEN.

I ask not human greatness,
  I ask not wealth or fame:
I only ask my soul renewed
  And sealed with Jesus's name.
To be an heir of heaven
  And have a mansion there,
Oh, there is naught of earthly good
  Can with such bliss compare.

I love the world of glory—
  There would I have my home.
Its pearly gates, its streets of gold,
  I long to call my own.
Its gentle stream of pleasure
  Where living waters roll,
With many a sweet attraction
  To win my thirsty soul.

That land of undimmed brightness,
  Hath blessed charms for me.

I like not skies where shadows fall,—
  But light eternally.
The gems which there are gleaming
  How brilliant do they shine!
Jasper and sapphire, precious stones
  Angelic brows entwine.

But all their beaming splendour
  Is borrowed from their king,
His smile gives brightness to that world,
  His love the seraphs sing.
I love that land of beauty;
  His peace is always there—
And always tones of melody,
  Are floating on the air.
Mrs. Mary B. Croker.

EXTRACT.

O fainting soul, arise and sing!
Mount, but be sober on the wing.
Mount up! for heaven is won by prayer;
Be sober, for thou art not there
Till death the weary spirit free;
Thy God hath said 'tis good for thee
To walk by faith and not by sight.
Take it on trust a little while,—
Soon shalt thou read the mystery right
In the full sunshine of his smile.
John Keble.

READY.

Oh to be ready
   When death shall come!
Oh to be ready
   To hasten home!
No earthward clinging,
   No lingering gaze,
No strife at parting,
   No sore amaze.
No chains to sever
   That earth has twined,
No spell to loosen
   That love would bind—
No flitting shadow
   To dim its light
Of the angel pinions
   Winged for flight.
But sweetly, gently,
   To pass away
From the world's dim twilight
   Into day!

Anon.

LILIES OF THE FIELD.

Lo, the lilies of the field!
How their leaves instruction yield!
Hark to Nature's lesson, given
By the blessed birds of heaven!—

Every bush and tufted tree
Warbles sweet philosophy :—
"Mortal, fly from doubt and sorrow,
God provideth for the morrow!"

Say, with richer crimson glows
The kingly mantle than the rose?
Say, have kings more wholesome fare
Than we poor citizens of air?
Barns nor hoarded grain have we,
Yet we carol merrily.
Mortal fly from doubt and sorrow,
God provideth for the morrow.

One there lives whose guardian eye,
Guides our humble destiny:
One there lives, who Lord of all,
Keeps our feathers, lest they fall:
Pass we blithely, then the time,
Fearless of the square and line,
Free from doubt and faithless sorrow;—
"God provideth for the morrow."

BISHOP HEBER.

TIME.

TIME is flying, flying,
  Oh how swiftly by!
Like a waterfall, that rushing,
Or a fountain, ever gushing—

Hourly, daily, weekly, yearly,
Rapid as the lightning nearly,
  Do the moments fly!

Catch the seconds, as they're passing,
  Wait not for the hours;
Prize them as a golden treasure—
Use them not in trifling pleasure—
Seconds, minutes, prizing, holding,
As you would those buds, unfolding
  Into choicest flowers.

Act for some important purpose,—
  Not with selfish zeal;
See,—humanity is bleeding,—
Aid thy fellow-man is needing;
Hundreds, thousands, millions, hear them
Breathing out their woes; go near them,—
  Seek their wounds to heal.

Soon another year all freighted
  With the deeds of man,
Will be borne to God, the giver,
And recalled by mortal never!
Oh be wakeful, watchful, ready,
Heart and hand to bless the needy;
  Thus fill out thy span.

Anon.

"THE TIME IS SHORT."

1 Cor. vii. 29.

Yes! our griefs will soon be over,
   Yes, our work will soon be done;
Every sunset brings us nearer
   To the never-setting sun.

Every parting hastes the meeting
   Of the inseparable band:
Onward, through the vale of weeping,
   We journey to the tearless land.

Thou, of love and zeal the giver,
   Jesus! grant us our request;
Let our life be full of labour,
   Calm and glorious our rest!

Written by a Theological Student of Geneva.

TRUST.

I'll spare all useless thinking,
Nor shall my soul be shrinking,
   Concerning what may be:
I'll follow thy kind leading;
Dear Lord in each proceeding,
   That thou art all, sufficeth me.

Anon.

"I AM READY TO FLY."

Ready now to spread my pinions,
    Glad to wing my flight away,
From the gloom that hovers round me
    To the realms of endless day.
Ready am I, washed and pardoned;
    Ready am I, freed from sin;
Ready to complete the conflict;
    Ready heavenly joy to win;—

Ready over death to triumph,
    And to tread the tempter down;
Ready life and bliss to inherit,
    And to wear the glorious crown;
Ready to be freed from sorrow,
    Tears and parting, toil and pain;
Ready for the heavenly mansion—
    Life is dear, but death is gain;—

Ready to forsake the shadows
    Of the night so dim and long;
Ready for my harp of glory;
    Ready for the angel's song;
Ready with salvation's banner,
    To ecstatic joys to rise;
Ready for the glad hosanna
    In the heavenly paradise;
Ready, with the just made perfect,
    Clothed in robes of life to be,

Swelling the enraptured chorus,
   Singing, joy and victory.

Heavenly messengers are round me;
   Hark! their voices bid me come;—
"Earth and time too long have bound thee;
   Sister spirit, welcome home."
Glad I go, my toil is finished;
   Broke at last my earthly spell;
Upward, now, my soul is tending—
   Earth, and time, and death, farewell!
Anon.

GOD APPOINTS.

Is thy lot lonely? fear it not, for He
Who marks the sparrow's fall, is guiding thee;
And not a star shines o'er thy head by night,
But He doth know that it will meet thy sight;
And not a joy doth beautify thy lot,
But tells thee still that thou art unforgot.
Nay, not a grief can darken or surprise,
Dwell in thy heart, or dim with tears thine eyes,
But it is sent, in mercy, and in love,
To bid thy helplessness seek strength above.
Anon.

"ONLY WAITING."

A very aged Christian, who was so poor as to be in an almshouse, was asked what he was doing now. He replied, "Only waiting."

Only waiting till the shadows
  Are a little longer grown;
Only waiting, till the glimmer
  Of the day's last beam is flown;
Till the night of earth is faded
  From the heart once full of day;
Till the stars of heaven are breaking
  Through the twilight soft and gray.

Only waiting till the reapers
  Have the last sheaf gathered home;
For the summer-time is faded,
  And the autumn winds have come.
Quickly, reapers, gather quickly
  The last ripe hours of my heart,
For the bloom of life is withered,
  And I hasten to depart.

Only waiting till the angels
  Open wide the mystic gate,
At whose feet I long have lingered,
  Weary, poor, and desolate.
Even now I hear the footsteps,
  And their voices, far away;

If they call me, I am waiting,
  Only waiting to obey.

Only waiting till the shadows
  Are a little longer grown;
Only waiting till the glimmer
  Of the day's last beam is flown;
Then from out the gathered darkness
  Holy, deathless stars shall rise,
By whose light my soul shall gladly
  Tread its pathway to the skies.

Anon.

NOTHING BUT LEAVES.

Nothing but leaves; the spirit grieves
  Over a wasted life;
Sin committed while conscience slept,
Promises made, but never kept,
  Hatred, battle, and strife;
    Nothing but leaves!

Nothing but leaves; no garnered sheaves
  Of life's fair ripened grain;
Words, idle words, for earnest deeds;
We sow our seeds—lo! tares and weeds;
  We reap, with toil and pain,
    Nothing but leaves.

Nothing but leaves; memory weaves
  No veil to screen the past;
As we retrace our weary way,
Counting each lost and misspent day,
  We find sadly at last
    Nothing but leaves.

And shall we meet the Master so,
  Bearing our withered leaves?
The Saviour looks for perfect fruit—
We stand before him humble, mute,
  Waiting the word he breathes—
    "Nothing but leaves."

Christian Inquirer.

FIRST AND LAST.

'Tis first the true, and then the beautiful;
  Not first the beautiful, and then the true:
First the wild moor, with rock and reed and pool,
  Then the gay garden, rich in scent and hue.

Not first the glad, and then the sorrowful;
  But first the sorrowful, and then the glad;
Tears for a day, for earth of tears is full;
  Then we forget that we were ever sad.

Not first the bright, and after that the dark;
  But first the dark, and after that the bright:
First the thick cloud, and then the rainbow's arch;
  First the dark grave, then resurrection light.

'Tis first the night—stern night of storm and war,
  Long night of heavy clouds and veiled skies;
Then the fair sparkle of the Morning Star,
  That bids the saint awake, and day arise.

HORATIUS BONAR.

GOD WILL SUPPORT.

HALF a wreck, by tempests driven,
  Yet this feeble bark survives;
Dashed against the rocks, and riven,
  In the midst of death it lives.
See it pressed on every side,
See it still the storm outride.

Can a bark like mine, so shattered,
  Ever reach yon friendly shore?
Tempest-tossed so long, and battered,
  Can it stand one conflict more?
Should another storm assail
Masts, and planks, and all, must fail.

So they would; but One that's greater
  Than the storms and waves, is here;
He it is whose name is sweeter
  Far than music to my ear.
Trusting in his grace and power,
Need I fear the darkest hour?

Anon.

HEAVEN.

That clime is not like this dull clime of ours;
    All, all is brightness there;
A sweeter influence breathes around its bowers,
    And a far milder air.
No calm below is like that calm above;
No region here is like that realm of love;
Earth's softest spring ne'er shed so soft a light;
Earth's brightest summer never shone so bright.

That sky is not, like this sad sky of ours,
    Tinged with earth's change and care;
No shadow dims it, and no rain-cloud lowers;
    No broken sunshine there!
One everlasting stretch of azure pours
Its stainless splendour o'er those sinless shores;
For there Jehovah reigns with heavenly ray,
There Jesus reigns, dispensing endless day.

The dwellers there are not like those of earth—
    No mortal stain they bear;
And yet they seem of kindred blood and birth,—
    Whence and how came they there?
Earth was their native soil; from sin and shame
Through tribulation they to glory came;
Bond slaves, delivered from sin's crushing load,
Brands, plucked from burning, by the hand of God.

Those robes of theirs are not like those below;
    No angel's half so bright!

Whence came that beauty, whence that living glow?
    Whence came that radiant white?
Washed in the blood of the atoning Lamb,
Fair as the light, those robes of theirs became;
And now, all tears wiped off from every eye,
They wander where the freshest pastures lie,
Through all the nightless day of that unfading sky.
HORATIUS BONAR.

A LITTLE WHILE.

BEYOND the smiling and the weeping,
    I shall be soon;
Beyond the waking and the sleeping,
Beyond the sowing and the reaping,
    I shall be soon.
    Love, rest, and home!
      Sweet home!
    Lord, tarry not, but come!

Beyond the blooming and the fading
    I shall be soon;
Beyond the shining and the shading,
Beyond the hoping and the dreading,
    I shall be soon.
    Love, rest, and home!
      Sweet home!
    Lord, tarry not, but come!

Beyond the rising and the setting
    I shall be soon;
Beyond the calming and the fretting,
Beyond remembering and forgetting,
    I shall be soon.
    Love, rest, and home!
      Sweet home!
    Lord, tarry not, but come!

Beyond the parting and the meeting
    I shall be soon;
Beyond the farewell and the greeting,
Beyond the pulse's fever beating,
    I shall be soon.
    Love, rest, and home!
      Sweet home!
    Lord, tarry not, but come!

Beyond the frost-chain and the fever
    I shall be soon;
Beyond the rock-waste and the river,
Beyond the ever and the never,
    I shall be soon.
    Love, rest, and home,
      Sweet home!
    Lord, tarry not, but come!
                HORATIUS BONAR.

ASPIRATIONS.

Purer yet, and purer,
  I would be in mind,
Dearer yet, and dearer,
  Every duty find.

Hoping still, and trusting
  God without a fear,
Patiently believing,
  He will make all clear.

Calmer yet, and calmer
  Trial bear, and pain,
Surer yet, and surer,
  Peace at last to gain.

Suffering still, and doing,
  To my lot resigned,
And to right subduing
  Heart and will and mind.

Higher yet, and higher,
  Out of clouds and night,
Nearer yet, and nearer,
  Rise towards the light.

Light serene and holy,
  Where my soul may rest,
Purified and lowly,
  Sanctified and blest.

Quicker yet, and quicker,
    Ever onwards press,
Firmer yet, and firmer,
    Step, as I progress.

Oft these earnest longings
    Swell within my breast,
Yet their inner meaning
    Scarce can be expressed.

Anon.

LEAD ME.

Oh! lead me in thy perfect way,
    Guide of my youth,—
From this time forth; and lest I stray,
Vouchsafe thine own unerring way,
    Spirit of Truth!

At thine omnipotent control
    Rude tempests cease—
Thou mak'st the broken spirit whole,
Oh! shed thy calmness on my soul,
    Spirit of Peace!

Oh! make me humble and resigned
    Beneath thy rod;
For thou art merciful and kind;
Exalt and purify my mind,
    Spirit of God.

Anon.

HE CHANGETH NOT.

I will never, never, leave thee,
   I will never thee forsake,—
I will guide, and save, and keep thee
   For my name, and mercy's sake;
      Fear no evil,
   Only all my counsel take.

When the storm is raging round thee,
   Call on me in humble prayer;
I will fold my arms about thee,
   Guard thee with the tenderest care,
      In the trial,
   I will make thy pathway clear.

When thy sky above is glowing,
   And around thee all is bright,
Pleasure, like a river flowing,
   All things tending to delight,
      I'll be with thee,
   I will guide thy steps aright.

When thy soul is dark and clouded,
   Filled with doubt, and grief, and care,
Through the mists by which 'tis shrouded,
   I will make a light appear,
      And the banner
   Of my love, I will uprear.

Thou may'st leave my care and keeping,
    Thou may'st wander far from me;—
Sorrow, then, and woe, and weeping,
    Mercy must mete out to thee:
        To the righteous
My rich blessings all are free.

When thy feeble flame is dying,
    And thy soul about to soar,
To that land, where pain and sighing
    Shall be heard, and known no more,
        I will teach thee
To rejoice that life is o'er!

Anon.

"COME UP HITHER."
Rev. iv. 4.

I shine in the light of God,
    His likeness stamps my brow,
Through the valley of death my feet have trod,
    And I reign in glory now.
No breaking heart is here,
    No keen and thrilling pain,
No wasted cheek, where the frequent tear
    Has rolled, and left its stain.

I have found the joy of heaven,
    I am one of the angel band,
To my head a crown is given,
    And a harp is in my hand.

I have learned the song they sing,
  Whom Jesus hath made free,
And the glorious walls on high still ring
  With my new-born melody.

No sin—no grief—no pain—
  Safe in my happy home—
My fears all fled—my doubts all slain—
  My hour of triumph come—
Oh friend of my mortal years!
  The trusted and the tried;
Thou art walking still in the valley of tears,
  But I am at thy side.

Do I forget? Oh no!
  For Memory's golden chain
Shall bind my heart to the heart below,
  Till they meet and touch again;
Each link is strong and bright,
  And love's electric flame
Flows freely down, like a river of light,
  To the world from which I came.

Do you mourn when another star
  Shines out from the glittering sky?
Do you weep when the noise of war
  And the rage of conflict die?
Then why should your tears roll down,
  And your heart be sorely riven,
For another gem in the Saviour's crown,
  And another soul in heaven?

                    ANON.

THE GUIDING HAND.

"Is this the way, my Father?" "'Tis, my child.
Thou must pass through this tangled, dreary wild,
If thou would'st reach the city undefiled,
      Thy peaceful home above."

"But enemies are round!" "Yes, child, I know,
That where thou least expectest, there's a foe;
But victor thou shalt prove o'er all below,—
      Only seek strength above."

"My Father, it is dark!" "Child, take my hand,
Cling close to me; I'll lead thee through the land;
Trust my all-seeing care; so shalt thou stand
      'Midst glory bright above."

"My footsteps seem to slide!" "Child, only raise
Thine eye to mine, then in these slippery ways,
I will hold up thy goings; thou shalt praise
      Me for each step above."

"O Father, I am weary!" "Lean thy head
Upon my breast. It was my love that spread
Thy rugged path: hope on, till I have said,
      Rest, rest, for aye, above!"
                           Anon.

HEAVEN.

No sickness there—
No weary wasting of the frame away—
No fearful shrinking from the midnight air,
No dread of Summer's bright and fervid ray.

No hidden grief;
No wild, and cheerless vision of despair,—
No vain petition for a swift relief—
No tearful eyes, no broken hearts are there!

Care has no home;
In the bright realms of ceaseless prayer and song
Its billows melt away, and break in foam
Far from the mansion of the spirit throng.

The storm's black wing
Is never spread athwart celestial skies,—
Its wailings blend not with the voice of spring,
As some too tender flow'ret fades and dies.

No night distills
Its chilling dews upon the tender frame;
No morn is needed there,—the light which fills
That land of glory, from its Maker came.

No parted friends
O'er mournful recollections have to weep;—
No bed of death, enduring love attends,
To watch the coming of a pulseless sleep.

No blasted flower—
Or withered bud, celestial gardens know;
No scorching blast, or fierce descending shower
Scatters destruction like a ruthless foe.

No battled word
Startles the sacred host with fear and dread.
The song of peace, creation's morning knew,
Is sung, wherever angel minstrels tread.

Let us depart,—
If home like this await the weary soul.
Look up, then, stricken one,—thy wounded heart
Shall bleed no more at sorrow's stern control.

With Faith our guide,
White-robed, and innocent, to lead the way,
Why fear to plunge in sorrow's rolling tide
And find the Ocean of Eternal Day?

Anon.

LIVING AND DYING.

I am not afraid of dying—
When the midnight winds are sighing;
I could beckon them to bear me, bear me to the upper skies.
And when the moon has risen
From her cloudy eastern prison,
I could sink with her at morning, nor wish again to rise.

Earth, with charms I cannot number,
  Woos me to a placid slumber.
Dreamless, deep, and all unbroken 'neath the summer turf, so green.
  Roses everywhere are blowing;—
  Will a better time for going
To the land of sleep and silence, come, life's morn and eve between?

  I am not afraid of dying
  In such holy quiet lying,
There would come no weary waking, with a weight upon my breast;
  Were the mornings gray or golden,
  By a sweet enchantment holden
I should slumber, till the angels bore me up to heavenly rest.

  But, O God! 'tis fearful *living*
  When we know each hour is giving
Radiance or shadows to the soul's eternal years.
  All my heart grows faint with sorrow;—
  Will it come,—the dim to-morrow,—
Bringing gladness, or the burden of to-day's o'erhanging fears?

  Mine's a short and simple story,
  Oh! thou tender Lord of glory!
Bear me gently in thy bosom, when I'm weary of the way.

Only let me see thee clearer,
Only whisper, "Child, come nearer,"—
So my *living* shall be blessed as my welcome *dying* day.

Anon.

THE MEETING PLACE.

Where the faded flower shall freshen—
  Freshen never more to fade;
Where the shaded sky shall brighten—
  Brighten never more to shade;
Where the sun-blaze never scorches;
  Where the star-beams cease to chill;
Where no tempest stirs the echoes
  Of the wood, or wave, or hill;
Where the morn shall wake in gladness,
  And the noon the joy prolong;
Where the day-light dies in fragrance,
  'Mid the burst of holy song;—
Brother, we shall meet and rest
'Mid the holy and the blest.

Where no shadow shall bewilder,
  Where life's vain parade is o'er;
Where the sleep of sin is broken,
  And the dreamer dreams no more:
Where the bond is never severed—
  Partings, claspings, sobs, and moans,

Midnight waking, twilight weeping,
  Heavy noon-tide—all are done;
Where the child has found its mother,
  Where the mother finds the child;
Where dear families are gathered,
  That were scattered on the wild;—
Brother, we shall meet and rest
'Mid the holy and the blest!

Where the hidden wound is healed,
  Where the blighted life re-blooms,
Where the smitten heart the freshness
  Of its buoyant youth resumes;
Where the love that here we lavish
  On the withering leaves of time
Shall have fadeless flowers to fix on,
  In an ever spring-bright clime;
Where we find the joy of loving
  As we never loved before—
Loving on, unchilled, unhindered,
  Loving once, and evermore;—
Brother, we shall meet and rest
'Mid the holy and the blest.

Where a blasted world shall brighten
  Underneath a bluer sphere,
And a softer, gentler sunshine,
  Shed its healing splendour here;
Where earth's barren vales shall blossom
  Putting on her robe of green,

And a purer, fairer Eden
  Be where only wastes have been;
Where a King, in kingly glory
  Such as earth has never known,
Shall assume the righteous sceptre,
  Claim, and wear the holy crown;—
Brother, we shall meet and rest
'Mid the holy and the blest."

HORATIUS BONAR.

OUR BELOVED HAVE DEPARTED.

Our beloved have departed,
While we tarry broken-hearted,
  In the dreary, empty house;
They have ended life's brief story,
They have reached the home of glory
  Over death victorious!

Hush that sobbing, weep more lightly,
On we travel, daily, nightly,
  To the rest that they have found,—
Are we not upon the river,
Sailing fast, to meet for ever,
  On more holy, happy ground?

On we haste, to home invited,
There with friends to be united

In a surer bond than here;
Meeting soon, and met for ever!—
Glorious hope, forsake us never,
For thy glimmering light is dear.

Ah! the way is shining clearer,
As we journey ever nearer
To the everlasting home.
Comrades, who await our landing,
Friends, who round the throne are standing,
We salute you, and we come.

From the German of Lange.

FOR WHOM SHOULD WE WEEP?

Weep not for those whose race is run;
Their prize is gained, their toil is done;
To them the power of grief is gone,
And misery's storm has frowned its last.
They sleep in Christ, the sleep of peace,
Unflushed by dreams of earthly sorrow,
Till earthly days and nights shall cease
Before a bright and glorious morrow.

But weep for those that yet remain,
The feverish weight of life sustaining,
The frown of scorn, the sting of pain,
And secret anguish uncomplaining.

Weep for the living; they who rest
    Within their last and happiest dwelling,
Are senseless of the vain bequest
    Of tears and sighs successive swelling.

Weep o'er the cradle,—not the tomb;
    Lament the dawn, and not the ending,
Of that tempestuous day of gloom,
    Whose sun is bright but when descending.
Weep for the bands who still maintain
    The strife, with labour undiminished.
Departed saints! their death is gain,
    Their spoils are reaped, their conflict finished.
Anon.

"THE REALMS OF THE BLEST."

We speak of the realms of the blest,
Of that country so bright, and so fair,
And oft are its glories confessed,
But what *must it be to be there?*

We speak of its pathways of gold,
Of its walks decked with jewels so rare;
Of its wonders and pleasures untold,—
But what *must it be to be there?*

We speak of its freedom from sin,
From sorrow, temptation, and care,
From trials without and within,
But what *must it be to be there?*

We speak of its service of love
Of the robes which the glorified wear,
Of the church of the first-born above,—
But what must *it* be to be there?

Do thou, Lord, 'midst sorrow and woe,
Still for heaven my spirit prepare;
And shortly, I also shall know
And feel what it *is* to be there?

Anon.

DAILY WORK.

In the name of God advancing,
  Sow thy seed at morning light,
Cheerily the furrows turning,
  Labour on, with all thy might.
Look not to the far-off future,
  Do the work which nearest lies;
Sow thou must before thou reapest,
  Rest at last is labour's prize.

Standing still is dangerous ever,
  Toil is meant for Christians now;
Let there be, when evening cometh,
  Honest sweat upon thy brow:
And the Master shall come smiling
  When work stops, at set of sun,
Saying, as he pays thy wages,
  "Good and faithful man, well done!"

From the German.

EVENING PRAYER.

I come to Thee to-night,
In my lone closet, where no eye can see,
And dare to crave an interview with Thee,
    Father of love and light!

Softly the moonbeams shine
On the still branches of the shadowy trees,
While all sweet sounds of evening on the breeze,
    Steal through the slumbering vine.

Thou gav'st the calm repose
That rests on all—the air, the birds, the flower,
The human spirit in its weary hour,
    Now at the bright day's close.

'Tis nature's time for prayer;
The silent praises of the glorious sky,
And the earth's orisons, profound and high,
    To heaven their breathings bear.

With them my soul would bend
In humble reverence at thy holy throne,
Trusting the merits of thy Son alone
    Thy sceptre to extend.

If I this day have striven
With thy blest Spirit, or have bowed the knee
To aught of earth in weak idolatry,
    I pray to be forgiven.

If in my heart has been
An unforgiving thought, or word, or look,
Though deep the malice which I scarce could brook,
    Wash me from the dark sin.

If I have turned away
From grief or suffering which I might relieve,
Careless the cup of water e'en to give,
    Forgive me, Lord, I pray.

And teach me how to feel
My sinful wanderings with a deeper smart,
And more of mercy and of grace impart,
    My sinfulness to heal.

Father, my soul would be
Pure as the drops of eve's unsullied dew,
And as the stars, whose mighty course is true,
    So would I be to thee.

Not for myself alone,
Would I these blessings of thy love implore,
But for each penitent the wide world o'er,
    Whom thou hast called thine own.

And for my heart's best friends,
Whose steadfast kindness o'er my painful years
Has watched to soothe afflictions, griefs, and tears,
    My warmest prayer ascends.

Should o'er their path decline
The light of gladness, or of hope, or health,

Be thou their solace, and their joy and wealth,
    As they have long been mine.

    And now, O Father, take
The heart I cast with humble faith on thee,
And cleanse its depths from each impurity,
    For my Redeemer's sake.
Hymns of the Ages.

HERE AND THERE.

What no human eye hath seen,
    What no mortal ear hath heard,
What on thought hath never been
    In her noblest flights conferred,
This hath God prepared in store,
For his people evermore.

When the shaded pilgrim-land
    Fades before my closing eye,
Then, revealed on either hand,
    Heaven's own scenery shall lie;
Then the vale of flesh shall fall,
Now concealing, dark'ning all.

Heavenly landscapes, calmly bright,
    Life's pure river, murmuring low,
Forms of loveliness and light
    Lost to earth long time ago,
Yes, my own, lamented long,
Shine amid the angel throng!

Many a joyful sight was given,
  Many a lovely vision here,
Hill and vale, and starry even,
  Friendship's smile, affliction's tear,
These were shadows sent in love,
Of realities above.

When upon my wearied ear,
  Earth's last echoes faintly die,
Then shall angel harps draw near,
  All the chorus of the sky;
Long-hushed voices blend again
Sweetly in that welcome strain.

Here were sweet and varied tones,
  Bird and breeze, and fountain's fall:
Yet creation's travail groans
  Ever sadly sighed through all;
There no discord jars the air—
Harmony is perfect there!

When this aching heart shall rest,
  All its busy pulses o'er,
From her mortal robes undrest,
  Shall my spirit upward soar;
Then shall pure, unmingled joy
All my thoughts and powers employ.

Here devotion's healing balm
  Often came to soothe my breast;
Hours of deep and holy calm,
  Earnests of eternal rest;

But the bliss was here unknown
Which shall there be "all" my own.

Jesus reigns, the Life, the Sun,
   Of that wondrous land above;
All the clouds and storms are gone,
   All is light, and all is love.
All the shadows melt away
In the blaze of perfect day.
From the German of Lange.

CHRISTIAN DUTY.

To be the thing we seem;
To do the thing we deem
   Enjoined by duty;
To walk in faith, nor dream
Of questioning God's scheme
   Of truth and beauty;

Casting self-love aside;
Discarding human pride,
   Our hearts to measure:
In humble hope to bide
Each change in fortune's tide
   At God's good pleasure;

To trust, although deceived;
Tell truth, though not believed,
    Falsehood disdaining;
Patient of ills received,
To pardon when aggrieved,
    Passion restraining;

With love no wrongs can chill,
To save, unwearied still,
    The weak from falling,—
This is to do God's will
On earth, and to fulfil
    Our heavenly calling.

      HORACE POETICA.

WORK AND REST.

WHAT have I yet to do?
    Day weareth on—
Flowers that, opening new,
Smile through the morning's dew,
    Droop in the sun.

Neath the sun's scorching glare,
    Fainting I stand;
Still is the sultry air,
Silentness everywhere
    Through the hot land.

Yet must I labour still,
    All the day through—
Striving with earnest will,
Patience my place to fill,
    My work to do.

Long though my task may be,
    Cometh the end.
God 'tis that helpeth me,
This is the work, and He
    New strength will lend.

He will direct my feet,
    Strengthen my hand;
Give me my portion meet;
Firm in his promise sweet,
    Trusting I'll stand.

Up, then, to work again!
    God's word is given,
That none shall sow in vain,
But find his ripened grain
    Garnered in heaven.

Larger the shadows fall,
    Night cometh on;
Low voices softly call,
"Come, here is rest for all!
    Labour is done!"

Anon.

LOSING AND LIVING.

For ever the sun is pouring his gold
  On a hundred worlds that beg and borrow;
His warmth he squanders on summits cold,
  His wealth on the homes of want and sorrow.
To withhold his largess of precious light,
Is to bury himself in eternal night:
    To give
    Is to live.

The flower shines not for itself at all,
  Its joy is the joy it freely diffuses;
Of beauty and balm it is prodigal,
  And it lives in the life it sweetly loses.
No choice for the rose but glory or doom—
To exhale or smother, to wither or bloom:
    To deny
    Is to die.

The seas lend silvery rain to the land,
  The land its sapphire streams to the ocean;
The heart sends blood to the brain of command,
  The brain to the heart its lightning motion:
And ever and ever we yield our breath—
Till the mirror is dry, and images death:
    To live
    Is to give.

He is dead, whose hand is not opened wide
   To help the need of a human brother;
He doubles the life of his life-long ride,
   Who gives his fortunate place to another;
And a thousand million lives are his
Who carries the world in his sympathies:
        To deny
        Is to die.

Throw gold to the far-dispersing wave,
   And your ships sail home with tons of treasure;
Care not for comfort; all hardships brave,
   And evening and age shall sup with pleasure;
Fling health to the sunshine, wind and rain,
And roses shall come to the cheek again:
        To give
        Is to live.

What is our life? Is it wealth and strength?
   If we for the Master's sake will lose it,
We shall find it a hundred-fold at length,
   While they shall for ever lose who refuse it;
And nations that save their union and peace
At the cost of right, their woe shall increase:
        They save
        A grave.

                                Anon.

I LOVE THEE.

Oh, how I fear Thee, living God!
    With deepest, tenderest fears!
And worship Thee, with trembling hope,
    And penitential tears!

Yet I may love Thee too, O Lord!
    Almighty as Thou art,
For Thou hast stooped to ask from me
    The love of my poor heart!

Oh then, this worse than worthless heart
    In pity deign to take,
And make it love Thee for Thyself,
    And for thy glory's sake.

No earthly father loves like Thee;
    No mother, half so mild,
Bears and forbears as Thou hast done,
    With me, thy sinful child!

Only to sit and think of God,
    Oh! what a joy it is!
To think the thought, to breathe the name,
    Earth has no higher bliss!

Father of Jesus! Love's Reward!
    What rapture will it be,
Prostrate before thy throne to lie,
    And gaze and gaze on Thee!

                FREDERICK FABER.

"TILL HE COME."

"Till He come"—Oh! let the words
  Linger on the trembling chords;
Let the little while between
In their golden light be seen;
Let us think how heaven and home
Lie beyond that—"Till He come."

When the weary ones we love
Enter on their rest above,
Seems the earth so poor and vast,
All our life-joy overcast?
Hush, be every murmur dumb—
It is only—"Till He come."

Clouds and conflicts round us press;
Would we have one sorrow less?
All the sharpness of the cross,
All that tells the world is loss,
Death, and darkness and the tomb,
Only whisper—"Till He come!"

See the feast of love is spread,
Drink the wine, and break the bread;
Sweet memorials—till the Lord
Call us round his heavenly board;
Some from earth, from glory some,
Severed only—"Till He come!"

Rev. E. H. Bickersteth.

THE WISH OF TO-DAY.

I ask not now for gold to gild
  With mocking shine a weary frame;
The yearning of the mind is stilled—
  I ask not now for fame:

A rose-cloud, dimly seen above,
  Melting in heaven's blue depths away—
Oh! sweet, fond dream of human love!
  For thee I may not pray.

But, bowed in lowliness of mind,
  I make my humble wishes known—
I only ask a will resigned,
  O Father, to thine own!

To-day, beneath thy chastening eye,
  I crave alone for peace and rest,
Submissive in thy hand to lie,
  And feel that it is best!

A marvel seems the universe,
  A miracle our life and death;
A mystery which I cannot pierce,
  Around, above, beneath.

In vain I task my aching brain,
  In vain the sage's thought I scan;
I only feel how weak and vain,
  How poor and blind, is man!

And now my spirit sighs for home,
   And longs for light, whereby to see;
And, like a weary child, would come,
   O Father, unto Thee!

Though oft, like letters traced on sand,
   My weak resolves have passed away,
In mercy lend thy helping hand
   Unto my prayer to-day!
JOHN G. WHITTIER.

PRAYER OF PATIENCE.

I am old and blind!
   Men point at me as smitten by God's frown;
Afflicted and deserted of my kind,
   Yet am I not cast down.

I am weak, yet strong;
   I murmur not that I no longer see;
Poor, old, and helpless, I the more belong
   Father Supreme, to Thee!

All-merciful One!
   When men are farthest, then art thou most near;
When friends pass by my weaknesses to shun,
   Thy chariot I hear.

Thy glorious face
  Is leaning toward me, and its holy light
Shines in upon my lonely dwelling-place—
    And there is no more night.

On my bended knee,
  I recognize Thy purpose, clearly shown;
My vision Thou hast dimmed that I may see
    Thyself—Thyself alone.

I have nought to fear;
  This darkness is **the shadow of thy** wing;
Beneath it I am almost sacred—here
    Can come no evil thing.

Oh! I seem to stand
  Trembling, where foot of mortal ne'er hath
    been,
Wrapped in that radiance from the sinless land,
    Which eye hath never seen.

Visions come and go,
  Shapes of resplendent beauty round me throng,
From angel lips I seem to hear the flow
    Of soft and holy song.

In a purer clime,
  My being fills with rapture—waves of thought
Roll in upon my spirit—strains sublime
    Break over me unsought.

Give me now my lyre!
  I feel the stirrings of a gift divine;
Within my bosom glows unearthly fire,
  Lit by no skill of mine!

Elizabeth Lloyd.

JOY.

Dear little child! with thy golden hair,
With thy rounded cheek, and thy brow so fair;
With thy ringing laugh, and thy sparkling eye,
Of a brighter hue than the cloudless sky,—
As thou dancest about in thy childish glee,
Thou seemest an emblem of joy to me.

But now, as thou playest—upon the wall
I mark that thy shadow doth softly fall;
Quickly thou runnest, yet near thy side,
Still doth that darkened outline glide,
It follows thee closely, from spot to spot,
And thou canst not move where it cometh not.

Oh joy! sweet joy! it is ever so;
There is ever some shade on thy path below;
Some thought of gloom, when our hours are
    brightest,
Some grief that comes when our hearts are
    lightest,

Some sadness that will on our spirits fall
As the shadow is thrown on the sunlit wall!

Should it not teach us to look away
From this world to the land of fadeless day,
Where sin and sorrow no entrance find,
And pleasure leaves no regret behind?
Banished for ever are clouds of care,
And joy is without its shadow there!

Anon.

GOD KNOWS IT ALL.

In the dim recess of thy spirit's chamber,
  Is there some hidden grief thou may'st not tell?
Let not thy heart forsake thee; but remember
  His pitying eye, who sees and knows it well.
            God knows it all!

And art thou tossed on billows of temptation,
  And wouldst do good, but evil oft prevails?
Oh think amid the waves of tribulation,
  When earthly hope, when earthly refuge fails—
            God knows it all!

And dost thou sin? thy deed of shame concealing,
  In some dark spot no human eye can see!

Then walk in pride, without one sigh revealing
　The deep remorse that should disquiet thee?
　　　　　　　　God knows it all!

Art thou oppressed and poor and heavy-hearted,
　The heaven above thee in thick clouds arrayed;
And well nigh crushed—no earthly strength imparted,
　No friendly voice to say—"Be not afraid?"
　　　　　　　　God knows it all!

Art thou a mourner? are thy tear-drops flowing
　For one too early lost to earth and thee?
The depths of grief no human spirit knowing;
　Which moan in secret, like the moaning sea—
　　　　　　　　God knows it all!

Dost thou look back upon a life of sinning?
　Forward, and tremble for thy future lot?
There's One who sees the end from the beginning,
　Thy tear of penitence is unforgot.
　　　　　　　　God knows it all!

Then go to God! Pour out your hearts before Him!
　There is no grief your Father cannot feel.
And let your grateful songs of praise adore Him—
　To save, forgive, and every wound to heal.
　　　　　　God knows it all—God knows it all!
　　　　　　　　　　Puritan Recorder.

MY CROSS.

"For my thoughts are not your thoughts, saith the Lord."
—Isa. lv. 8.

"For I know the thoughts that I think towards you—
thoughts of peace and not of evil, to give you an expected
end."—Jer. xxix. 11.

And when that happy time shall come of peace and rest,
We shall look back upon our path, and say—*It was the best.*

It was a time of sadness—and my heart,
Although it knew and loved the better part,
Felt wearied with the conflict and the strife,
And all the needful discipline of life.

And while I thought on these—as given to me,
My trial tests of faith and love to be,
It seemed as if I never could be sure
That faithful to the end I should endure.

And thus, no longer trusting to His might,
Who says, "We walk by faith, and not by sight;"
Doubting, and almost yielding to despair,
The thought arose—*My cross I cannot bear.*

Far heavier its weight must surely be,
Than those of others which I daily see;
Oh, if I might another burden choose,
Methinks I should not fear my crown to lose.

A solemn silence reigned on all around,
E'en nature's voices uttered not a sound;

The evening shadows seemed of peace to tell,
And sleep upon my weary spirit fell.

A moment's pause—and then a heavenly light
Beamed full upon my wondering sight,
Angels on silvery wings seemed everywhere,
And angel's music thrilled the balmy air.

Then One, more fair than all the rest to see,
One—to whom all others bowed the knee—
Came gently to me, as I trembling lay,
And,—"Follow me," he said; "I am the way."

Then speaking thus, he led me far above,
And there beneath a canopy of love,
Crosses of divers shape and size were seen,
Larger and smaller than mine own had been.

And one there was, most beauteous to behold,
A little one, with jewels set in gold—
Ah! this, methinks, I can with comfort wear,
For it will be an easy one to bear.

And so the little cross I quickly took,
But all at once my frame beneath it shook;
The sparkling jewels, fair they were to *see*,
But far too heavy was their *weight* for me.

"This may not be," I cried, and looked again
To see if there were any here could ease my pain,
But one by one I passed them slowly by,
Till on a lovely one I cast my eye.

17 *

Fair flowers around its sculptured form entwined,
And grace and beauty seemed in it combined;
Wondering I gazed—and still I wondered more
To think so many should have passed it o'er.

But oh! that form, so beautiful to see,
Soon made its hidden sorrows known to me;
Thorns lay beneath those flowers and colours fair,
Sorrowing, I said, "This cross I may not bear."

And so it was with each and all around,
Not one to suit my *need* could there be found,
Weeping, I laid each heavy burden down,
As my Guide gently said, "No cross,—no crown."

At length to Him I raised my saddened heart;
He knew its sorrow, bade its doubts depart—
"Be not afraid," **he** said, "but trust in me,
My perfect love shall now be shown to thee."

And then with lightened eyes and willing feet,
Again I turned, my earthly cross to meet,
With forward footsteps, turning not aside,
For fear some hidden evil might betide.

And there, in the prepared appointed way,
Listening to hear, and ready to obey,
A cross I quickly found, of plainest form,
With only words **of** love inscribed thereon.

With thankfulness I raised it from the rest,
And joyfully acknowledged it the best—

The *only* one of all the many there,
That I could feel was *good* for me to bear.

And while I thus my chosen one confessed,
I saw a heavenly brightness on it rest;
And as I bent—my burden to sustain—
I recognized my own old cross again!

But oh, how different did it seem to be!
Now I had learned its preciousness to see;
No longer could I unbelieving say,
"Perhaps another is a better way."

Ah, no! henceforth my one desire shall be,
That He who knows me best should choose for me,
And so whate'er his love sees good to send,
I'll trust; it's best—because He knows the end.
Anon.

I SHALL BE SATISFIED.

Not here! not here! not where the sparkling waters
  Fade into mocking sands as we draw near;
Where in the wilderness each footstep falters—
  I shall be satisfied—but oh! not here.

Not here! where every dream of bliss deceives us,
  Where the worn spirit never gains its goal;

Where haunted ever by the thoughts that grieve us,
  Across us floods of bitter memory roll.

There is a land where every pulse is thrilling
  With rapture earth's sojourners may not know,
Where Heaven's repose the weary heart is stilling,
  And peacefully life's time-tossed currents flow.

Far out of sight, while yet the flesh enfolds us,
  Lies the fair country where our hearts abide,
And of its bliss is naught more wondrous told us,
  Than these few words, "I shall be satisfied."

Satisfied! satisfied! the spirit's yearning
  For sweet companionship with kindred minds,
The silent love that here meets no returning—
  The inspiration which no language finds.

Shall they be satisfied? the soul's vague longings—
  The aching void which nothing earthly fills?—
Oh! what desires upon my soul are thronging,
  As I look upward to the heavenly hills!

Thither my weak and weary steps are tending—
  Saviour and Lord! with thy frail child abide!
Guide me towards home, where all my wanderings
    ending,
  I then shall see Thee, and "be satisfied!"

Congregationalist.

WORDS.

Words are lighter than the cloud foam
    Of the restless ocean spray;
Vainer than the trembling shadow,
    That the next hour steals away.
By the fall of summer rain-drops
    Is the air as deeply stirred;
And the rose-leaf that we tread on
    Will outlive a word.

Yet on the dull silence breaking,
    With a lightning flash, a word,
Bearing endless desolation
    On its slighting wings, I heard.
Earth can forge no keener weapon,
    Dealing surer death and pain,
And the cruel echo answered,
    Through long years again.

I have known one word hang star-like
    O'er a dreary waste of years,
And it only shone the brighter
    Looked at through a mist of tears,
While a weary wanderer gathered
    Hope and heart on life's dark way,
By its faithful promise shining,
    Clearer day by day.

I have known a spirit calmer
  Than the calmest lake, and clear
As the heavens that gazed upon it,
  With no wave of hope or fear.
But a storm had swept across it,
  And its deepest depths were stirred,
Never, never more to slumber,
  Only **by a** word.

I have known a word more gentle
  Than the breath of summer air,
In a listening heart it nestled,
  And it lived for ever there.
Not the beating of its prison
  Stirred it ever night or day;
Only with the heart's last throbbing
  Could it fade away.

Words are mighty, words are living;
  Serpents, with their venomed stings;
Or bright angels, crowding round us
  With heaven's light upon their wings;
Every word has its own spirit,
  True or false, that never dies;
Every word man's lips have uttered
  Echoes in God's skies.

Household Words.

HE LEADS HIS OWN.

"I will lead them in paths they have not known."—
Isaiah xlii. 16.

How few, who, from their youthful day,
   Look on to what their life may be,
Painting the visions of the way
   In colours soft, and bright, and free;
How few, who to such paths have brought
The hopes and dreams of early thought!
For God, through ways they have not known,
        Will lead his own.

The eager hearts, the souls of fire,
   Who pant to toil for God and man,
And view with eyes of keen desire
   The upland way of toil and pain;
Almost with scorn they think of rest,
Of holy calm, of tranquil breast,
But God, through ways they have not known,
        Will lead his own.

A lowlier task on them is laid,
   With love to make the labour light;
And there their beauty they must shed,
   On quiet homes, and lost to sight.
Changed are their visions, high and fair,
Yet calm and still they labour there;
For God, through ways they have not known,
        Will lead his own.

The gentle heart, that thinks with **pain,**
  It scarce can lowliest tasks fulfil,
And, if it dared its life to scan,
  Would ask but pathway low and still;
Often such lowly heart is brought
To act with power beyond its thought;
For God, through ways they have not known,
      Will lead his own.

And they, the bright, who long to prove,
  In joyous path, in cloudless lot,
How fresh from earth their grateful love
  Can spring, without a stain or spot;—
Often such youthful heart is given,
The path of grief to walk to heaven;
For God, through ways they have not known,
      Will lead his own.

What matter, where the path may be?
  The end is clear and bright to view;
We know that **we a** strength shall see,
  Whate'er the day may bring **to** do,
We see the end, the house of God,
But not the path to that abode;
For God, through ways they have not known,
      Will lead his own.

Hymns of the Ages.

HYMN.

There is no pain that I can bear,
    But thou, my God, hast borne it;
No robe of scorn that I can wear,
    But thou, my Lord, hast worn it.

There's no temptation I endure,
    But thou, my King, endured it;
There's not a wound that asks a cure,
    But my Redeemer cured it.

For me, thy sacred temples bled;
    For me, thou wert upbraided;
"And as a lamb to slaughter led,"
    Unpitied and unaided.

And can I doubt thy tender love?
    Thy rich compassion—doubt it?
My spirit hath no hope above,
    "No stay on earth without it."

Anon.

WAIT.

Wait! for the day is breaking,
    Though the dull night be long;
Wait! God is not forsaking
    Thy heart. Be strong—be strong!

Wait! and the clouds of sorrow
  Shall melt in gentle showers,
And hues from heaven shall borrow,
  As they fall amidst the flowers.

Wait! 'tis the key to pleasure
  And to the plan of God;
Oh, tarry thou his leisure—
  Thy soul shall bear no load!

Wait! for the time is hasting
  When life shall be made clear,
And all who know heart-wasting
  Shall feel that God is dear.

          CHAUNCEY HARE TOWNSHEND.

ENDURANCE.

"If thou faint in the day of adversity, thy strength is small."—Prov. xxiv. 10.

FAINT not beneath thy burden, tho' it seem
  Too heavy for thee, and thy strength is small;
Tho' the fierce raging of the noon-tide beam
  On thy defenceless head untempered fall.

Tho' sad and heart-sick with the weight of woe,
  That to the earth would crush thee—journey on;
What tho' it be with faltering steps and slow,
  Thou wilt forget the toil when rest is won!

Nay, murmur not, because no kindred heart
   May share thy burden with thee—but alone
Still struggle bravely on, tho' all depart;
   Is it not said that "each must bear his own?"

All have not equally the power to bless;
   And of the many, few could cheer our lot;
For "the heart knoweth its own bitterness,"
   And with its joy a stranger meddleth not.

Then be not faithless, tho' thy heart be dark,
   Is not thy Master's seal upon thy brow?
Oft has his presence saved thy sinking bark;
   And thinkest thou He will forsake thee now?

Hath he not bid thee cast on Him thy care,
   Saying, He careth for thee? Then arise!
And on thy path, if trod in faith and prayer,
   The thorns shall turn to flowers of Paradise.
                                 Anon.

ANGELS.

Oh never, till the clouds of time
   Have vanished from the ken of man,
And he, from yonder heaven sublime
   Looks back where mystic life began,
Will gathered saints in glory know
What blessings men to angels owe!

This earth is but a thorny wild,
  A tangled maze where griefs abound;
By sorrow vexed, by sin defiled,
  Where foes and friends our walk surround,
But does not God in mercy say,
Angelic guardians line the way?

Sickness and woe perchance may have
  Ethereal hosts whom none perceive,
Whose golden wings around us wave,
  When all alone men seem to grieve:
But while we sigh, or shed the tear,
Their sympathies may linger near.

When gracious beams of holy light
  From heaven's half-opened portals play,
And from our scene of suffering night
  Melts nigh its haunted gloom away;
Each doubt, perchance, some angel sees,
And hovers o'er our bended knees.

And when at length this weary life
  Of toil and danger breathes its last,
Or ere the flesh with parting strife,
  Is down to clay and coldness cast,
The struggling soul may learn the story
How angels waft the blest to glory.

JAMES MONTGOMERY.

OUR HOURS ARE ANGELS.

Each hour is like an angel, that with wings,
    Comes from, and goes to heaven; yet empty
        ne'er.
Comes or returns, but some occasion brings,
    And hastens back to heaven, the tale to bear
    Of evil, or fresh store to treasure there.

Wrestle, as with an angel, with each hour,
    And hold him; though he seem a child of air,
Yet he will, in the struggle, give thee power,
And, though the flesh grows weak, will leave a
        heavenly dower.
                  JOHN G. WHITTIER.

THE SLEEP.

    "He giveth his beloved sleep."—Psalm cxxvii.

Of all the thoughts of God that are
Borne inward unto souls afar,
    Along the Psalmist's music deep—
Now tell me, if there any is,
For gift or grace surpassing this,
    "He giveth His beloved sleep."

What would we give to our beloved?
The hero's heart to be unmoved—
　The poet's star-tuned harp to sweep—
The senate's shout to patriot vows—
The monarch's crown to light the brows?—
　"He giveth *His* beloved sleep."

What do we give to our beloved?
A little faith, all undisproved,
　A little dust to overweep—
And bitter memories to make
The whole earth blasted for our sake!
　"He giveth His beloved sleep."

"Sleep soft, beloved!" we sometimes say,
But have no tune to charm away
　Sad dreams, that through the eyelids creep;
But never doleful dream again
Shall break the happy slumber when
　"He giveth His beloved sleep."

O earth, so full of dreary noises!
O men, with wailing in your voices!
　O delved gold, the wailer's heap!
O strife, O curse, that o'er it fall!
God makes a silence through you all,
　And "giveth His beloved sleep."

His dew drops mutely on the hill;
His cloud above it smileth still,
　Though on its slope men toil and reap;

More softly than the dew is shed,
Or cloud is floated overhead,
  "He giveth His beloved sleep."

Ha! men may wonder while they scan
A living, thinking, feeling man,
  In such a rest his heart to keep;
But angels say—and through the word
I ween their blessed smile is *heard*—
  "He giveth His beloved sleep!"

For me, my heart, that erst did go,
Most like a tired child at a show,
  That sees through tears the juggler's leap—
Would now its wearied vision close,
Would childlike on *His* love repose,
  Who "giveth His beloved sleep!"

And friends, dear friends, when it shall be
That this low breath has gone from me,
  And round my bier ye come to weep,
Let me, most loving of you all,
Say, not a tear must o'er her fall—
  "He giveth His beloved sleep!"
Mrs. Elizabeth Barrett Browning.

MISSION OF THE ANGEL OF DEATH.

"Go forth," said the heavenly Father,
  To one of his seraph train;
"Go forth on an errand of mercy,
  To the world of trouble and pain.

"Loosen the galling fetters
 That bind the weary and worn;
And bear to their glorious mansions
 The souls that for bliss are born.

"And away from earth's noxious vapours,
 Some buds of beauty bring,
To bloom in the heavenly gardens,
 'Neath the smile of perpetual spring."

And the angel, with wings resplendent,
 Went out from the heavenly band,
'Midst a chorus of joyful voices,
 Resounding at God's right hand.

In the street of a crowded city,
 An old man beggared and poor,
Hungry and sick and sorrowing,
 Sank down by a rich man's door.

Sleep weighed down his heavy eye-lids,
 And feebly he drew his breath,
As beside him, with look of compassion,
 Alighted the angel of death.

Then he thought of the years long vanished,
 The lovely, the lost, and the dear,
Till borne on the wings of sweet vision
 He woke in a happier sphere.

FOR HEAVY HEARTS.

There were none on earth to sorrow,
    That the old man's days were o'er,
But myriads bade him welcome,
    As he neared the heavenly shore.

Slowly night's gathering shadows
    Closed round a mother mild,
Who, tearful and heavy-hearted,
    Watched by her dying child.

Fevered and restless and moaning,
    On his little bed he lay,
When the bright-winged angel drew near him,
    And kissed his last breath away.

So softly the chain was severed—
    So gently was stayed the breath—
It soothed the heart of the mourner,
    And she blessed the angel of death.

For she knew the soul of her darling
    Had gone to his Father above,
Clasped in the arms more tender
    Than even her fondest love.

And still on his holy mission
    Did the heaven-sent messenger roam,
Gathering God's wandering children
    To their eternal home.

Those only whose souls were blighted
  And withered by sin and shame,
Saw no light in the path of the angel,
  And knew not from whence he came!

And those only who close their spirits
  In wilful blindness here,
From the light of God's nearer presence
  Need shrink with distrust and fear.

Mrs. S. W. Jewett.

THE MORNING-GLORY.

We wreathed about our darling's head the morning-
  glory bright,
Her little face looked out beneath, so full of love
  and light,
So lit as with a sunrise, that we could only say,
She is the morning-glory true, and her poor types
  are they.

So always, from that happy time, we called her by
  their name,
And very fitting did it seem, for sure as morning
  came,
Behind her cradle-bars she smiled to catch the first
  faint ray
As from the trellis smiles the flower, and opens to
  the day.

But not so beautiful they rear their airy cups of
    blue,
As turned her sweet eyes to the light, brimmed
    with sleep's tender dew,
And not so close their tendrils fine round their sup-
    ports are thrown,
As those dear arms, whose out-stretched plea clasped
    all hearts to her own.

We used to think how she had come, even as comes
    the flower,
The last and perfect added gift to crown love's
    morning hour,
And how in her was imaged forth the love we could
    not say,
As on the little dew-drops round shines back the
    heart of day.

We never could have thought, O God, that she must
    wither up
Almost before a day was flown, like the morning-
    glory's cup;
We never thought to see her droop her fair and no-
    ble head,
Till she lay stretched before our eyes, wilted and
    cold and dead.

The morning-glory's blossoming will soon be com-
    ing round,
We see their rows of heart-shaped leaves uprising
    from the ground,

The tender things the winter killed, renew again
    their birth,
But the glory of our morning has passed away from
    earth.

O earth! in vain our aching eyes stretch over thy
    green plain,
Too harsh thy dews, too gross thine air, her spirit
    to sustain;
But up in groves of Paradise, full surely we shall
    see
Our Morning Glory, beautiful, twine round our dear
    Lord's knee.

                              MRS. LOWELL.

THE END.

www.ingramcontent.com/pod-product-compliance
Lightning Source LLC
Chambersburg PA
CBHW020815230426
43666CB00007B/1029